Celebration of

INDIAN Classical Dances

Priya Venkataraman

Celebration of INDIAN Classical Dances

Utpal K Banerjee

A Shubhi Publications Enterprise
Gurgaon - India

Shubhi Economy Editions
First Economy Edition - 2012

Published by
Shubhi Publications
240, 2nd floor, City Centre, Gurgaon - 122 002, Haryana, India

Photo Credits
Anurupa Roy, Ashwani Chopra, Avinash Pasricha, Deepak Mudgal, Geeta Chandran, ICCR, Invis Multimedia, Kalashram, Kiron Pasricha, Parwati Dutta, Priti Patel, Purva Dhanashree, Ranjana Gauhar, Sudha Grover, The International Centre for Kathakali (ICK), Uma Amtani, Urmimala Sarkar, Usha Kris

Designed by SN GRAPHIX

Printed in India by
Aegean Offset Printers
220-B, Udyog Kendra 1, Greater Noida
Uttar Pradesh-201306 (India)

Vijayalakshmi

Sharon Lowen

Bharati Shivaji

Reela Hota

Contents

PREFACE **11**

PART ONE – GENERAL **15**

PART TWO – CLASSICAL DANCES **33**

INTRODUCTION – Mrinalini V. Sarabhai 34

BHARATANATYAM *(Overview: Rama Vaidyanathan)* *41*

ODISSI *(Overview: Madhavi Mudgal)* *99*

KATHAK *(Overview: Saswati Sen)* *121*

MANIPURI *(Overview: Singhajit Singh)* *159*

KATHAKALI *(Overview: Deepti Omcheri Bhalla)* *167*

MOHINIYATTAM *(Overview: Jayaprabha Menon)* *177*

KUCHIPUDI *(Overview: Vanashree Rao)* *187*

VILASINI NATYAM

(Overview: Anupama Kylash and Sanjay Kumar Joshi) *193*

SATTRIYA DANCE *(Overview: Indira PP Bora)* *203*

CHHAU (*Overview: Shashi Dharan Nair)* *213*

PART THREE – MEDLEY AND MISCELLANY **221**

Bibliography 239

Index 241

Gopika Verma

Preface

There have been few civilisations whose mythic memory is redolent with dance, where principal gods are dancers: Shiva as *Nataraj* and Krishna as *Natabar,* — when whole heavens resonate with the ethereal music from the other deities like Saraswati and even sages like Narada. In the Greek mythology major gods are all evanescent and only Jupiter's daughters make the minor deities as Nine Muses for the performing arts. Bharata's *Natya Shastra* caries forward a litany of *Margi* and *Desi* that, in effect, is a consolidation of the then prevailing classical and regional forms of dance, among others, and the legacy is still much alive after over two millennia.

Around Independence, the resurrection and resuscitation of Indian classical and contemporary dances have been an extraordinary phenomenon. What was languishing especially in the previous century and just about surviving in the quarters of courtesans and in the temples in the hands of god's maids – the virtual torch-bearers of a decaying heritage – got a fresh lease of life and connoisseurs gave them flesh and blood. The major form of Bharatanatyam and an exhilarating form of contemporary dance were both given fresh energy simultaneously in the South by Rukmini Devi Arundale and in the north by Uday Shankar, while in the East, Tagore gave dulcet touch to his complete dance-dramas; and all these happened remarkably together in the time-frame of the 1930's. Post-Independence, while the momentum gathered for the other seven recognised genres of classical dances, contemporary styles did not progress much after Shankar's passing away in the 70's. There has been enviable progress, on the whole, in the entire dance arena in the recent years and *Gurukul* traditions have continued to flourish. This book is an illustrative recapitulation of the throbbing dance-scene of today, with many glimpses provided and insights offered. It begins with the classical dance scenario and, after a brief introduction, takes up each of the eight forms: Bharatanatyam, Kathak, Kathakali, Kuchipudi, Manipuri, Mohiniyattam, Odissi and Sattriya, — with Chhau and Vilasininatyam, thrown in for good measure, as they seem to be deserving contenders for classical status. For each form, an Overview has been given by a young practitioner who has really the 'pulse' of their own genre!

The author is especially thankful to the great scholar-choreographer-danseuse Mrinalini Sarabhai for her very special contribution. The author is also beholden to the thirteen young professional gurus, choreographers and danseuses – from the eight recognized classical forms, and the two newly-noticed forms of Vilasininatyam and Chhau — who have unstintedly offered their critical overviews in their own domains. They are: the noted young Bharatanatyam dancer Rama Vaidyanathan; the doyen of Odissi dance, Madhavi Mudgal; the celebrated Kathak danseuse, Saswati Sen; the revered guru of Manipuri dance, Singhajit Singh; the dancer-choreographer and Kathakali scholar, Professor Deepti Omcherri Bhalla; the well-known young Mohiniyattam dancer Jayaprabha Menon; the celebrated Kuchipudi dancer Vanashree Rao; the pioneer Sattriya dancer, Indira PP Bora; the newly-emerging Vilasininatyam dancers, Dr. Anupama Kylash and Sanjay Kumar Joshi; and the talented Chhau dancer-choreographer Shashi Dharan Nair.

It was considered important to incorporate their overviews in their own professional areas: to gain an insight and share it with the reader, alongside some instances of what is happening in each individual genre. All critical illustrations are to provide glimpses into what is happening and, howsoever illustrative (and not attempted to be comprehensive) should whet the reader's appetite for more. Images have been added – again with the help of the dancers themselves and by noted photographers.. Most of all, it is Avinash Pasricha whose eloquent camera has provided a lively dialogue with the professionals whose works are critiqued here, — to get a glimpse of their creative mind. A new dimension is added by the outstanding Kathak dancer-cum-illustrator Raghav Raj Bhatt, whose sketches on all forms of dances are an innovative delight.

— UTPAL K BANERJEE

Chitralekha

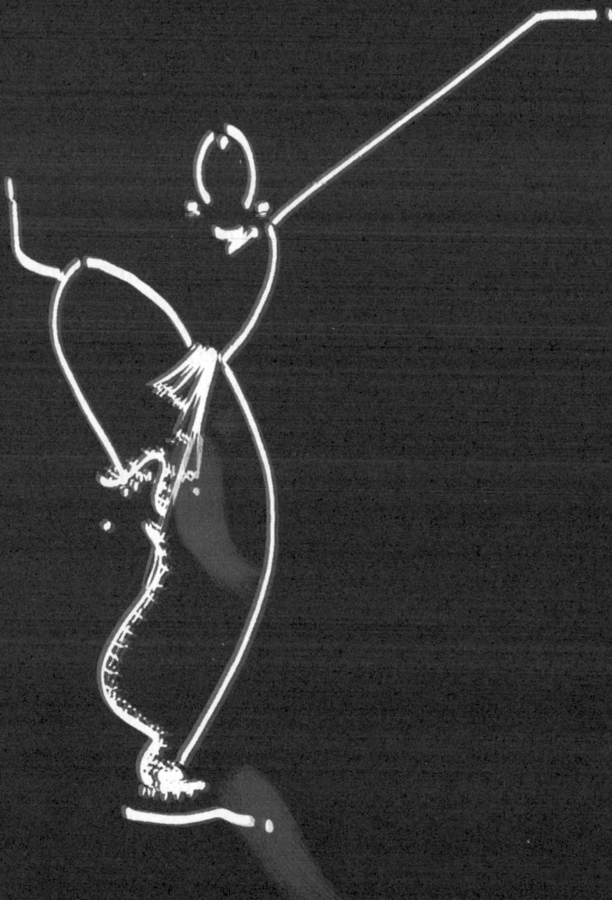

General

BOUNDARY AND BEYOND: *Some Significant Events*

Recent years have been extraordinarily eventful for dance in India. Hardly the centenary birth-celebrations of Rukmini Devi Arundale — the progenitor of Kalakshetra who single-handedly resuscitated the Bharatanatyam style — were over, when the dance world suffered the body-blow of Kelucharan Mahapatra's demise. Till the advent of his eighties, Kelubabu had been crafting the Odissi genre: to give it the shining luminescence and global presence that it so richly deserved. The nation gave him a last, tearful salutation. M S Subbulakshmi's was another departure that reeled the cultural cognoscenti, from north and south alike.

Youth has been on the ascendant in the countless evening soirees, flocking to see performances and following them up by joining dance classes all over the city. "Dance is such an essential and integral part of our culture that I'm glad that the present generation is flocking by droves to our training sessions", exclaims a visibly happy Raja Reddy whose annual, half-week *Parampara* festivals have become a permanent fixture in the country's culture calendar. "Dance, like cricket, needs opportunity to show its innovative side. After I'd used our President's patriotic poem to be visualised in dance, I've received numerous requests from college students and their principals for creating group choreography in English language!" While classical dances have doubtless come to stay, the modern dance scene has not been so active and alive. Says Narendra Sharma (whose recent demise was a cultural shock), the last disciple of Uday Shankar and doyen of the contemporary dance-theatre, "Creative dance is

Mallika Sarabhai

the poor cousin of the whole dance world! Barring a few sporadic attempts, it has not yet got its due."

On the creative front, perhaps the most venerable voice in the terpsichorean world is that of Mrinalini Sarabhai who told this analyst-commentator, "I think I must swim with today's mainstream events, otherwise how can I keep alive?" on the occasion of releasing her well-documented autobiography *The Voice of the Heart,* the evening saw a delectable performance by three generations of Sarabhais: with Mrinalini, Mallika and the little Anahita dancing together. "I'm all for adding new dimensions to the classical styles. It should be like the poetry of Tagore and Eliot who are our contemporaries. I've performed on woman's forced divorce and dowry-death: based on pure dance-syllables!" Daughter Mallika, whose burning concerns for environment and humanism are well-known, conceived *Colours of the Heart* and joined hands with the explosive Saudi-Pakistani singing-talent Samia Malik to present a gripping performance on the Independence Day — using songs, dances and personal histories. Santosh Nair, the gifted Chhau and contemporary choreographer, presented *The Game of Dice,* from the Mahabharata, with innovative music composition and percussion effects.

Continuing with creativity, Tagore's dance persona had bloomed fairly late in his life and only by the 1930's did he arrive at his thematic dance dramas: with an organic commingling of the classical forms with the abundant folk traditions, blending them with the rhythmic *Kalasam* of Kathakali, virility of *Kandyan* dance from Sri Lanka and grafting of ritualistic dance elements from Bali, Java, Cambodia, Myanmar, China and Japan. Delhi ballet Group celebrated their golden jubilee under Guru Valmiki Banerjee and focused on what he termed *Rabindra Natyam,* — with a *margam* (sequence) of Tagore dances, set to his inexhaustible lyrics. Remi Srikant — a senior dancer from Gujarat – led her nine-member troupe to present *Maya,* which, according to her, could be "a dust storm, mirage, shadow, reflection, rain, birth, death, ghost or dream: anything intangible." Preeti Vasudevan from the USA produced *Strings Unattached,* a three-piece contemporary dance: as a dialogue process between ancient and modern texts, traditional Bharatanatyam and modern idiom, Indian Raga music and Western chamber music. Aditi Mangaldas, the Kathak Danseuse, who had earlier performed a highly innovative *Changing Landscapes – Textures of Passion,* set up a six-hour workshop later, led by Guru Kumudini Lakhia, aimed at metamorphosing the mindset of dancers. "Even a moment can change history", avers she. Shashidharan Nair, the ace choreographer behind SBKK's highly successful dance-dramas year after year, held forth to this analyst-commentator on the fundamentals of creative choreography: basics of footwork; building up of stamina; exercises for body flexibility and, finally, blending body movements, footwork and expressions.

On the classical front, Margi Sathi, accompanied by the resonant earth-drum Mizavu, presented one of the most traditional forms of Nangiyar Koothu, an offshoot of the 2000-year old Sanskrit drama Kudiyattam. From the same redolent breezes and swaying palms of Kerala came Mohiniyattam of Bharati Shivaji, presenting four generations of shared heritage, — using lilting devotional hymns from *Thiru Pavai,* a literary heritage from the Tamil post-*Sangam* era. Bharati's talented disciple Mom Ganguly brought a fresh sensibility in Mohiniyattam, wafting the *Ashtapadi* melodies from Jayadeva's *Geeta Govinda* as sung in Kerala temples.

From neighbourhood Tamil Nadu, Malavika Sarukkai carved sculptures in space with scintillating Bharatanatyam using her core concepts of *sthiti* (stillness) and *gati* (dynamism), in *Darshanam: A Vision.* The Canada-born Ginette Dion-Ahmed brought cross-cultural classicism in *Devi,* represented as the supreme feminine spirit worshipped at myriad levels. Saroja Vaidyanathan, a senior dancer, traced the origin of Bharata's *Natya Shastra*, beginning at the very beginning when gods fought demons and used many ploys to get nectar. The highly gifted Rama Vaidyanathan expounded the verse from *Taittriya Aranakyam: The world is made of water and it is the basis of everything and worthy of our prayers*. Another youthful dancer Maria Kiran, brought up by her adoptive parents in France, revealed her métier in Bharatanatyam, and positively seemed to be another Alarmel Valli in the making.

On the dance-drama front, *Kannappar Kuravanji,* part of a 300-year old oral tradition, was presented by Kalakshetra – about Shiva's ardent devotee Kannappar – to pay homage to Rukmini Devi. Their other offerings were *Maha pattabhishekam,* the grand finale of Rukmini Devi's impeccable Ramayana series and *Rukmini Ksalyanam,* her free adaptation from Andhra's *Bhagavata Mela Nataka* tradition. The other *Bhagavata mela*-trained young dancer from Chennai was N Srikanth, who excelled in *Stree Vesham* (women's garb).

The Karnataka-based Vyjayanthi Kashi brought alive the legacy of *Dharavu,* that harks back to *Dhruva Gana* of the 2nd century and is mentioned in *Natya Shastra,* in *Yakshagana* style. Swapna Sundari created the image of Devaki, Krishna's natural mother, who could only have a long-distance imagination from her solitary confinement. APJ Abdul Kalam's poetry, on *Vision of India,* transformed into Kuchipudi dance through Raja's expertise, brought tumultuous applause. Vilasininatyam is the lesser-known temple-based form from Andhra (unlike its secular sister form Kuchipudi) that is being revived by Swapna Sundari –with other scholars — and was brilliantly presented by the young Purva Dhanasree, with highly lyrical *abhinaya* (expression).

From the far northeast, Poushali Chatterjee of Kolkata brought in Manipuri style, — to perform with the US-based Sreyashi Dey; to

Sonal Mansingh

present *Lavanya.* Sreyashi is working to 'de-exoticise' Indian classical dance in the foreign shores and deserve praise. The other variation from the neighbouring Assam was Sattriya dance, now elevated to a classical form: by Indira Bora and her highly gifted daughter Menaka. *Khuman* (Black Sun), choreography in Manipuri form by Priti Patel, depicted contemporary Manipur: torn by strife and struggle.

Sonal Mansingh, one of the senior most danseuses, mixed Odissi with Chhau and other stylised forms, and presented many ideas. One was the *'K' Concept*, where she explored the adoration of the pastoral god, —amalgamating many legends, beliefs, rituals and festivals. At another, metaphysical level, she brought out how: "When you are up against adversity, you need correct intents which eventually lead to triumph: *Satyameva Jayate."* The US-born Odissi dancer Sharon Lowen and the Italy-born Ileana Citaristi – who, between them, combine 60 years of happy dancing in India – brought out many nuances and facets of the form, as honed by their celebrated guru Kelubabu. The other dancer Kiran Sehgal, a child prodigy from the old Prithvi theatre, demonstrated many aspects of symbolic energy coming to life and ending with ritual worship, — using even contemporary and folk styles. Sharmila Biswas from Kolkata worked out how classical Odissi evolved through the ages: not merely from folklore, Aryan advent and sanctity of temples; but also from handicrafts, costumes and musical instruments. A lesser-known Odissi guru was Pankaj Charan Das, whose grip on the feminine *Mahari ang* was supreme. This legacy was well illustrated by the US-based Ratna Roy, his only disciple, along with Scheherazade and Sitara.

Above all was the north's perennial favourite Kathak, presented splendidly by Geetanjali Lal, basing her choreography entirely on Carnatic music by G S Rajan. Another refreshing effort was by Amita Dutt from Kolkata, who picked up songs by the rebel poet Kazi Nazrul, a great favourite in both Bengals. An utmost novelty was to stage vintage Shakespeare through Kathak. Saswati Sen, the choreographer, also essayed the role of Juliet in a fun-filled *Romeo and Juliet.* Set to music by the redoubtable Birju Maharaj: using ragas like *Pahari, Durga, Kirwani* and *Bhairavi.* Lucknow-based danseuse Kumkum Dhar brought out the nuanced differences among the three gurus from there: Achchan Maharaj, Lachchu Maharaj and Shambhu Maharaj. Kumudini Lakhia established visually how attention should go beyond technique to the space around the dancers.

REVERBARATION OF DANCE-CADENZA: *World Dance Day — I*

Treatises on Indian classical arts conjure up a grand vision of the dance by Nataraja Shiva: where his is the dance of the cosmos, with the accompaniment of music of spheres and the accoutrement of the moon and the stars. While the World Dance day, observed every year on 29 April, brings its significance and relevance down to the present times, the ancient vision is as valid on mythological, metaphysical, ecological, aesthetic and even scientific grounds. There can be a meaningful poser: why do we dance the way we are accustomed, when there should be no 'today' in our dance?

Leela Venkataraman, a thoughtful commentator and analyst of the scene, covered thoroughly the state of Indian dance today. Performance of dancers has to negotiate different paths where the performer, in addition to be savvy in her art, be also her PR expert, organiser of programmes, adept with authorities and mindful of the infrastructure. In the complex role of dancer-performer-teacher-artiste, she is acutely aware of verities of life: with pain and pleasure of everyday occurrence. An astute observer like Uttara Asha Coorlawala hints half-jokingly to the Brahminisation of classical dance: depicting the dancer's body and limbs in a complete *Varnashram*! More seriously, there are today disciples galore of each dance-guru and still a maestro like Birju Maharaj has to lament that in the prevailing mediocrity that rules the roost, the interest is less in complete training than in learning 'items'.

Some significant innovative works are visible, such as, Swapna Sundari's revival of *Vilasini Natyam* from out of Devadasis of Andhra Pradesh, which is quite different from Kuchipudi or Bharatanatyam; Mahua Mukherjee's pioneering work on *Gaudiya Nritya* as Bengal's age-old tradition; and *Mayurbhanj Chhau* used in scores of dance-dramas, not imagined before. There are anomalies, too. While South Africa has several schools of Kuchipudi, Bharatanatyam and Odissi, halls in India go begging for dance-audience. Again, dancers seldom attend performances by others from the same fraternity.

On the whole, classical dances have distinct regional flavours. Odissi, for instance, has a song: *Kete Chhanda Janile Nandarajara Pilati*: that would need a good initiation into local idiom for adequate interpretation. Regional languages are like gates: to enter the verity of classical dance and attain universality. In seminar-discussions in Washington, DC on Odissi and in Chicago on Bharatanatyam, these points have been debated. The other moot point is the role of *Sahitya* and the intimacy of *Abhinaya* vis-à-vis pure *Nritta*. Cross-cultural endeavours are also visible today in Bharatanatyam, Kuchipudi, Odissi and other genres. One must be confident of one's identity and then interact with others. Navtej's *Fana'h* with Sufi music is an important work: mixing Bharatanatyam with Chhau and the contemporary, without drowning identity. Rohini Bhate's Kathak, using Marathi *Abhang*, is a case in point. A recent trend is using dance as a spectacle: with group dances from the traditional repertoire, as done in the Purana Qila ambience. The need not to lose the subtleties in the huge space remains valid, so that the spectacle does not become a razzmatazz!

Silence, a vital mode of communication, is often lost sight of, — with de-humanisation of quietude! There is also a relative lack of platform for virile male dancers, although Kuchipudi, Raas and *Shabda Nritya* were male bastions till quite late. The Gotipuas of Orissa, in fact, have a repertoire of some 300-400 songs, out of which only *Bandha Nritya* is extant. Navtej is, however, one exception with commendable work on urban design. Dance has been put to some social use. Devika has developed a dance-process for teaching and Astaad Deboo has used dance to involve the handicapped. Many teachers continue to be performers, which was not always the case earlier. Giving platform to young dancers remains another crucial necessity, with Priti Patel having done some god work: with a young dancers' festival. Many dancers have ceased to be self-centred and have worked with other disciplines, such as, Seema Agarwal's production of Meera and Geeta Chandran's work with puppetry.

Abhinaya is often so emasculated that only small auditoria in Delhi like IIC and Triveni can do it justice! Side by side, an *Abhinaya*-based item like *Padam* seems to have almost disappeared. Dance cannot surely be confined to only *Nritta*, as often executed in Kathak for hours! The other point is the absence of dialogue between dancers and dance-critics, — should they not occasionally come together? It is tragic to witness dancers beg for audience, without much regard for the art form. While one does not decry small islands of excellence and recognises that dancers struggle against many odds, there should be better ways of assessing merits and mark out good programmes, — even with some co-existence of mediocrity, concluded Leela.

On changing contours of dance presentation, Anita Ratnam — who has been running 'The Other Festival' for nearly a decade, in early December every year in Chennai before the onset of the month-long crowded events in *Sabhas* there — narrated how she has always to fall back upon her personal network. In trying to let innovative experiments happen with music plus theatre plus dance, new audiences are required, but difficult to come by: in the absence of 'marquee' names. One needs a formidable ability to take risks and make the festival itself the star! Using Chennai museum theatre, modelled on Shakespeare's Globe Theatre in London, bringing in school-audience and working out the logistics of empowering young people (often with barely 25 students) to manage art-events were areas discussed. Anita's other venture, the Website Narthaki.com, provides space for subversive voice on the Internet.

SPIC-MACAY is today a 30-year old unique service-forum: providing appreciation to classical arts in schools and colleges, — now extended to public parks. Covering audiences who may be unaware of the mystique and mythology of our traditions, and often vanguards of individual families, — it arranges lecture-demonstrations. For dance, the packaging may include costume, light and pre-recorded music, although live music is preferred. While fusions, now more than ever, may have resulted in some loss of soul, even Kudiyattam and Manipuri have reached remote corners. For volunteer-students, who run the shows, the compensation is in intangibles: like interaction with artistes as great human beings. Dance in the park in now in the offing.

The Habitat experience has been, over the last seven years, promotion of love and respect for the classical arts and inter-disciplinary fusion. Madhavi Mudgal, an eminent dancer-teacher, shared her thoughts on how tradition itself is changing with times. Indrani Rahman in olden times, for instance, would not hesitate to perform Kuchipudi, Odissi and Bharatanatyam in the course of the same evening, — with possibly the same accompaniment, something not done today. According to her, artistes are always born, only to be groomed by good gurus. Anita Singh, whose Patiala Festival is now a couple of decades' old, brought up the promotional aspects of a festival: by corporate bodies, by government and by ticket-buying public. While all three have their roles, the balance among them has been changing over locations and time. She, for one, has been promoting heritage sites at Patiala, Kapurthala and Amritsar, a worthy precedent for others – like corporate houses with means — to follow.

WHEN WORLD GOES TRAIPSING: *World Dance Day — II*

Communities of dancers and dance-enthusiasts, as stated earlier, celebrate World Dance Day on 29 April every year everywhere. Initiated in 1982 by International Dance Council (CID) of UNESCO, hand-in-hand with UNICEF, the UN body for children, the Day gives a clarion call to persons institutionally involved with dance – teachers, choreographers, group-leaders, media-persons, researchers, scholars and all associated organisations – to go out and catch attention of wider public to the art of dance. Accent is given on addressing 'new' persons who do not normally witness dance-events during the year. CID visualises Dance Day events as special performances, open-door courses, public rehearsals, lectures, exhibitions, stories in newspapers and magazines, dance-evenings, radio and TV programmes, visits street-shows, — organised primarily by dance companies, amateur groups, schools, associations and others active in dance. Dedicating one World Dance Day to children, declares Alkis Rafftis, President of CID, "Caring for children is the cornerstone of human progress. Dance is a basic component of personal and societal development, and no child should be left without the opportunity to learn and practise dance. Access to the art is a right for every person and children in particular…"

'Kalashram', the dream-institution of Kathak Maestro Birju Maharaj, and 'Natya Vriksha', the centre for classical dance-training under Geeta Chandran, came forward together to celebrate the Day. While Natya Vriksha invited the celebrated dancer, choreographer and activist Mrinalini Sarabhai, who heads 'Darpana' in Ahmedabad, to lecture to public on *Bhootam-Bhavyam-Bhavishyam*il and assess

World Dance Day 2007, Delhi

Indian classical dance through the prisms of yesterday, today and tomorrow, — Kalashram's plan was comprehensive, well-spread and more germane to the UNESCO manifesto. Says Saswati Sen, the moving spirit behind Kalashram, "We're holding *Yuva Kala Utsav*, a festival of dance music and painting by young artists. We've an adequate nucleus of 120+ students in our Mayur Vihar campus and 80+ in Jor Bagh who learn Kathak, Bharatanatyam and both vocal and instrumental music We'll take them to reach the masses and add our mite to the government's 0.05% budget on culture!"

The festival took off at Indira Gandhi Kala Kendra in NOIDA with a *Saraswati Stuti*, followed by Kathak solos and duets, by some 30 children in the age-groups: 6-8, 10-12 and 14-18. The venue shifted to Mekhala Jha auditorium of Bal Bhavan next day morning when the Kotla Road complex saw an 'on-the-spot' painting competition by young talents aged 5-18 years, divided into groups below and above 12 "We've massively publicised through schools, posters, banners and mass media," informs Saswati. There was an evening programme of vocal singing and some solos and duets, — again from junior and senior diploma-groups of youthful learners.

Walk for Art was an arresting feature on 29 April – tried only once earlier for the artist community by Raja-Radha Reddy's Kuchipudi centre under their daughter Yamini's infectious zest — that began from India Gate, reached Mandi House and returned to India Gate. "300-400 children walked, wearing artistic T-shirts, caps and hold placards. The choice of this route was because of its juxtaposition with cultural organisations like SBKK, Little Theatre Group, Triveni Kala Sangam, Sangeet Bharati and others, which the children were asked to identify. To add piquancy, we threw in a quiz programme – with attractive prizes – on the names of institutions, what they did and organisations they represented", points out Saswati.

The finale was a grand ballet *Wrana Rang* at Sathya Sai International Centre on day after, inspired By Tagore's noted poem *Hori Khela*. Unlike the earlier production by Mamata Shankar Ballet Group of Kolkata, the story-line here went further, as Saswati elaborates, "We started with a chess-game that the Pathans played against the Rajputs and, on the ruse of cheating, turned violent and kill the unarmed and unsuspecting Rajputs on the spot. Now in the spirit of revenge, the Rajputs conspired to use Hori as a festive game and drew the Pathans into revelry, — only to discard disguise later and kill them, as narrated by Tagore. We wanted to strengthen our theme with multiple games as conducive to youthful imagination and build choreography around them." With 55-60 awards thrown in, the Dance Day celebrations were great fun!

ODE TO WORLD DANCE: *World Dance Day — III*

Tagore wrote once: *The sudden flash of illumination brightened up my whole being*, — not necessarily pegged on any occasion. Kolkata could go gaga on the least provocation and the World Dance Day on

29 April provided the right spark. The marvellously placed culture-complex of 'Rabindra Sadan', 'Nandan' and 'Bangla Academy' came alive early on the sun-lit morning and saw visitors streaming, until the late evening reverberation of jingling feet finally faded away. Considering that the idea grew as a joint endeavour among the World Dance Alliance – Asia Pacific, West Bengal Dance Group Federation and West Bengal State Music Academy – besides EZCC and ICCR — the mammoth turn-out of viewers and performers alike came as no surprise.

Says Urmimala Sarkar, the prime force behind the effort, "We successfully celebrated the international event earlier in Kolkata and could bring together dancers, choreographers, teachers, dance enthusiasts, scholars and students. The event became important in highlighting dance-activities in West Bengal, especially keeping the young and enthusiastic new generation of dancers in mind." Adds she, "We hope to create an environment of sharing in larger multi-cultural contexts of the whole of Asia and the Pacific, — by becoming active participants in dance-related activities, of performances, dance workshops, seminars, young choreographers exchange programmes, organised or supported by World Dance Alliance – Asia Pacific."

The spirit of innovation that Kolkata dancers imbued came through characteristically from the documentary-tribute to Guru Govindan Kutty who passed way the other day. An accomplished Kathakali dancer-choreographer from Kerala Kalamandalam – under the nurturing care of its founder-poet Narayana Vallathol, he shifted to 'Darpana' of Ahmedabad as the Kathakali-partner of Mrinalini Sarabhai but, after a while, a restless soul brought him to Kolkata. He flourished here: not merely by teaching the classical forms to a large ensemble of students present on this occasion, but also performing himself in Tagore's *Valmiki Pratibha* and *Chitrangada*, using superlative Kathakali Mudras, — after completely forsaking

Kathakali's head-gears, face-paints and elaborate costume.. The result was electrifying and did ample justice to Tagore's imagination.

Among the morning groups, 'Behala Ragini' produced *Arghya* (Tribute) with a mix of Bharatanatyam and contemporary styles, to the music of Vishwa Mohan Bhatt, and 'Niharika Centre for Performing Arts' staged *Harmony* to an incomprehensible Latin American tune, 'Charaibeti' let loose assorted kids to produce *Shishu* (Child), while *Symphony of Spring* by 'Sapphires' was easily an original piece for its freezes and assemblages.

The evening showcased *Golden Mermaid* from Khmer Ramayana of Cambodia. The petite Chumvan Sodachivy in the eponymous role was hypnotic, — supported by Khiev Sovannarith as the universally-applauded monkey with wild antics. "Sanskritiki Sreyaskar' executed Tagore's rain-song: *Hail to my dark*, *handsome Lord*: in Kathak with pale-deep blue tunics and later came 'Ananda Shankar Group' with *Reincarnation*. Describes Tanushree Shankar, the latter's director, "I visualised a life-cycle from adolescence to old age, back to re-birth, in energised movements." 'Calcutta Dance Theatre' presented children of the future, followed by 'Hritaal' with another Tagore-song: *I'm the restless one, thirsting afar…*'Kanakangi' blended the classical with the contemporary, to Vikram Ghose's music, while 'Ranan' presented scintillating Kathak by Vikram Iyengar. 'Tarit Sarkar Ballet Troupe' presented

World Dance Day, Kolkata

Nilanjan to Nachiketa's gritty melodies, while Arnab Bandyopadhyay of 'Darpani' excelled in interpreting Tagore's lyric: *Oh the solemn One, resting in dark firmaments draped in azure-blue hues*...

The penultimate item was *Ritmos* ('Rhythm', in Portuguese), an ensemble work in four segments of rhythms and rhapsodies. Explains Emma Powell, the director who graduated from 'Australian Academy of Performing Arts', "I conducted a two-week, 20-participant workshop, with exposure to contemporary techniques and movements like slides, rolls and head-turnings: aimed at making body flexible at shoulders and hips." *Impact,* the finale, was another workshop-based presentation under Taiwan's I-Feng Tung, an established performer, choreographer and educator. Says Tung, "My youthful workshop concentrated on 'Lemon' technique, improvisation and impersonation: leading to contacts with and against each other. It was fun using video exposures and listening sessions: through minimalist music and electronic sounds." It was heart-warming to see the participants resonate to their Asia-Pacific mentors!

ART: *Alone And Aware*

It is illuminating to explore the mindset of a dancer and examine her stance vis-avis multiplicity of audiences in a fast-changing world. The young danseuse Geeta Chandran was approached as a spokesperson of today's dancing generation. She has been generally having a full slate of events, —meant for a wide variety of audience in different festivals, seminars and conferences. "While dance occupies the centre stage at these gatherings, the range of spectators is quite spectacular," avers Geeta. "I've to cater to different kinds of audience taste and take my art to suit each of the different settings."

Adds she, "It's the question of the whole attitude. Some are there to see the exotica; students are perhaps witnessing the form for the first time and take it as more of an education; others suffer ennui and have to be brought to the fold of *rasikas* (connoisseur). As a dancer, one has to update oneself and keep oneself intellectually alone and aware. We were not taught this in our upbringing. Let me be clear: some of my performances are need-based, while a few satisfy my creative urge. I've to adapt myself to the need-based ambience, — to external as well as internal pressures. Market forces are external, such as, duration of 40 minutes; emphasis on fast numbers; performance for group items alongside solos; etc. Internal pressures are the matching process: I must be able to communicate, — go this far and no further."

How much shall be an artist's adaptive ness to meet such diversity? "The art scene is changing rapidly," responds Geeta. "A lot of intellectual quest is happening. There is so much exploration in terms of music and thematic content. The earlier generation of dancers could do with *Margam* (set sequence). Today, either they appear as already seen before, or their new interpretation is not clear enough nor very distinctive. I'm not at all against traditional repertoire and there are forums for it. But there's a need for fresh formats, too and I need to expand my reach: in breadth and in depth. There is, for instance, an idea to dance alongside sculpture, which is growing on me for the last ten years. *Her Voice* is another item of mine, by collaborating with puppetry. Since it takes time to absorb and relate to a new idea, it's desirable to keep it alive for some time, — in order to let it grow well." On music, "It is my launch pad," says the dancer. "I'm also fond of an inspiring poetry, — by way or lyrics or English poems. Incidentally, what you see on stage is interesting, but what all you discard before reaching there is vital!" Commenting on dance as a profession, "Formal education gives one many choices. Hence, if

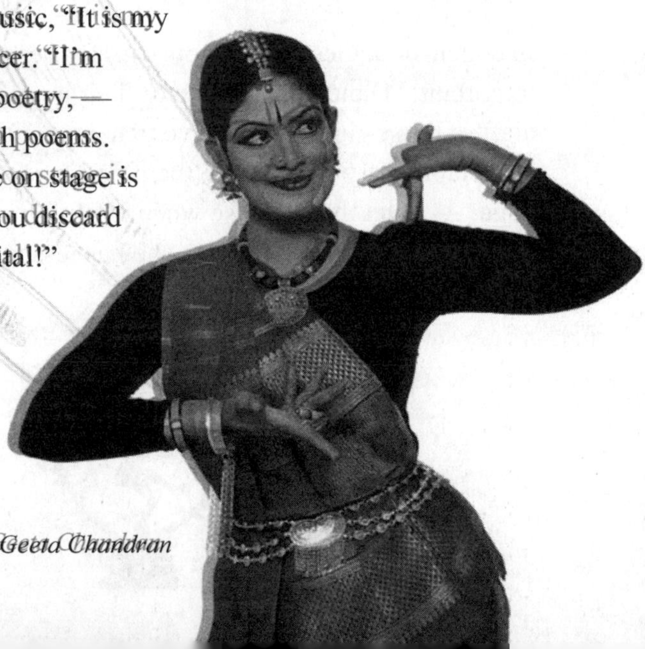

Geeta Chandran

one chooses dance, it is for an innate love for the art and knowledge of the canvas. This is unlike scions of some gurus, who were born to their art, — unless they were bright and worked really hard, they would remain mediocre as artistes. In contrast, today's generations, like mine, have known their mind and whatever art form they take up must reach another level and create new audience." About her upbringing, she explains, "I was part of the Lady Sriram College (LSR) crowd who would relate to beautiful poetry and paintings, and would express liking for my costumes, but nothing beyond! I resolved to break the barriers so that I could reach out to them. First, it was language. I explored Hindi lyrics and English poetry – when they were not so popular – and occasionally used flute in the background. Secondly, I used a changed format, — through concept-based items, to get out of the traditional straight-jacket. Thirdly, it was poetry: to be generally sensitive and especially to explore women's issues. Dance is an extension of one's personality and cannot be totally different on stage and off stage. Recently, I did an item at the British Council, based on Vidyapati, where Radha complains that Krishna is not satisfying her sexually. People found it different, yet acceptable. Fourthly, there were experiments in collaboration. I presented, for example, *Shivam* as an exploration of space by one male and three female dancers – rather than as group choreography – preceded by a poem written by Chandra Rajan and recited in the beginning."

In conclusion, Geeta points out that for her students, pedagogy is important. "Dance is only one of their many activities – like tennis, craft or horse-riding – and I've to devote quality time to make it acceptable. I try to sensitize them first, with music, mythology, yoga, — to let them realise when it's full moon or when the spring has come and gone!" Perhaps she has lessons for us all, even beyond dance!

Classical Dances

Mrinalini Sarabhai

Introduction

Bhootam – Bhavyam – Bhavishyam

Assessing Indian Classical Dance through the Prisms of Yesterday, Today and Tomorrow

by Mrinalini V. Sarabhai

The dance, like the ever-turbulent flowing sea, keeps moving and is never stagnant. There are many so-called traditionalists who talk of keeping a form 'in tact' and, if new ideas are introduced, are deeply critical. Yet, the programme of Bharatanatyam, as is presented now, is only about two hundred years old, though the form is ancient. So are many of the other dance techniques. From the beginning of time, nearly five thousand years in historical terms in India, the dance has been evolving, changing and exploring. For, the dance is the basic expression of man's aspirations. The fundamental source is the same; the motivation differs, as does the outward observable pattern.

In India, the dance structure is the tradition, the shape and style of the movements. Each region gave its own image to the dance, the people their inner aspirations; the individual teachers gave vent to the longing within the depths of their hearts. So, while the essential framework remained, the forms of dance changed. The great saint Bharata who gave us the valuable treatise, the *Natya Shastra*, speaks of gurus before him, whose works he has collected as basic contributions to his own compilation. Hindu philosophy, with its focus on the arts as reflecting the exuberant outburst of the soul's longing for God, became the background of dance compositions. In and around temples, the dance became an artistic expression of religious themes, and poets wrote songs extolling the deeds of the Divine Ones upon the earth, pouring their won ecstatic suffering into melodic compositions.

Bodily movement in every detail of expressive feeling took on a special significance, and organised disciplines slowly became the classical dance, as it is known today. Temple walls depict sculptures that bear close resemblance to the postures of the dance. It is possible to recognise and trace the origins of our rich inheritance. Gurus have constantly changed patterns according to their own gifts of perception. Patrons like the maharajas and nawabs, added their need for entertainment and scholastic knowledge to the existing forms. Kathak, for instance, was influenced by dancers from Persia, when they were brought here to dance at the fabulous courts of the Mughals. But, on the whole, the patterns of change were gentle and more perhaps a re-creation, with sophistication and understanding of the shapes of traditional norms. n our own century, there was Menaka, who experimented with the Kathak dance. There was Uday Sankar, whose bold works drew much from the folk techniques. In the south in Tamil Nadu, Rukmini Devi gave a chaste dignity to Bharatanaryam and Vallathol Menon, the poet of Kerala, gave new impetus to the art of Kathakali. In Bengal, Rabindranath Tagore brought the best of Manipuri teachers to his university at Santiniketan for his lyrical dance-dramas. These great artists all paved the way to the work we do today.

For me, from the moment I set foot on earth, dancing was my inheritance and I was possessed with the need to express my thoughts in kinetic movements. It took many years of hard training, working ten to twelve hours a day to reach a point where I could create works of my own. The first composition that perhaps could be noted as a personal experience was based on the life of man: *Manushya*. Before that there were several, but they still clung to already known themes. *Manushya* broke away from tradition though it used the basic technique of Kathakali, with new movements woven into the classical fabric. It dispensed with elaborate costumes and kept only the powerful simplicity of the style. Then came *Matsya Kanya* (the Fish Princess): a fairy tale, romantic and lyrical. No *mudras*, no elaborate *abhinaya,* just the dance: music with now words, movement in all the beauty of the Indian dance form. It was perhaps created to show that the body conveys deep meaning without the need of verbal explanation.

Through the years, there were many more. The pressure of the world in which we live has tremendous repercussions on the artist. The dance on a woman's 'dowry death' brought a contemporary theme to the dance world. It received an enormous amount of comment, even editorials referring to it and its impact on society. Suddenly, from being involved so much in social problems, I reacted and created the abstract *Song of Creation*, perhaps the first piece of its kind in India. It came from studying the Vedas and was danced in silence. Tantrik art had fascinated me long before it became fashionable and when *Maya and the Disciple* was presented in Paris, I met many scholars to discuss the philosophy and the art which was known to very few at the time. The theme was of a man who sought self-realisation through the Goddess. Each gesture and movement was symbolic and the man represented the created world, which always strives for the ultimate whole, the perfection of the Great Goddess. The colours used in the lighting were based on Tibetan *thankas*.

All my work naturally comes from the past. The technique, the heritage, the land, the environment: these are all within me. It is from this background, training, knowledge and experience that I draw. Then there is the present, which are our society, our culture, and our values. The artist spans the past and present, and dynamically thrusts both into the future when she speaks. Often what is accepted as beauty by tradition is dynamited by an artist. In *Manushya* I brought death onto the stage, not permitted by Bharata in his *Natya Shastra.*. In *Memory* the woman jumps to her death with a child in her arms.

In *Ashwathamma*, a modern reconstruction of the old story, Ashwathamma in strange ways is the victor, for, it is his wickedness that the world imitates. Often during a conversation an idea is caught, nurtured and then transfigured. A conversation on the atomic bomb with Vikram Sarabhai and his passionate conviction that it must be used only for peaceful purposes, started us both thinking of how modern life often replayed the old, how myths were repeated each century. This took me to the story of *Ashwathamma* and there it was. Ashwathamma sends out into the world the arrow of destruction, not knowing how to recall it. He too kills innocent citizens and young children, as did the perpetuations of Hiroshima and Nagasaki. It was the totality of man's continual struggle with his emotions the conflict of good and evil. Here words were needed, so a one-act play was added to the dance. The words at the end were significant. Ashwathamma asks 'Krishna, where are you? I am still here and these are all my children!'

The dancer constantly — with body, mind and spirit — affirms the meaning of life as she sees it. The body, fully trained, is a body that is free to express emotion. In India the detailed training of the dance technique is an extraordinary discipline: with years of hard work 'sadhana,' meaning years of freedom, to be able to become aware of the potential of the body: to express, to think in movement, the summation of all experience. To use the inner and the outer vision in wholeness that is both passionate and spiritual. In dance, the entire person is involved. Dance is comprehensive. 'Where the hand goes the eyes follow, where the eyes go the mind follows, where the mind goes the emotion follow,' says an old verse. Each work of mine has sprung from some deep chasm within myself, beginning as a thought and ending in an explosion! The period between is one of 'agony and ecstasy'. It is in this sudden moment of perception when all boundary lines of man and the universe disappear, that creativity is at its highest. It is a conceptualisation of the formation of the universe and its oneness with man: complete identity.

For instance, I had never even remotely thought of dancing Kalidasa's *Shakuntala*. What triggered off the obsession with the curse of Durvasa, I still do not know. Yet, suddenly it was heavy within me, the thought of predetermined action. Was a careless, thoughtless gesture purely accidental? Often the results were terrifying. Do we release some destructive thought knowingly? As upon the barren landscape by a painter, I placed the figures of the drama, each one to play its part alone and in togetherness with Shakuntala. Who is to blame for her rejection by Dushyanta, the king? The saint's curse is not only for the young maiden but also for everyone: Kanva, Anasuya, Priyamvada and Dushyanta. The progression of the plot is shown to the audience in episodes of individual reactions. Each one is to be blamed or perhaps to be blamed or perhaps to be pitied. Finally, Shakuntala rejects them all, goes on her way along. 'Alone we are born, alone we die'.

For months we rehearsed, I could not find an answer, for the ending. The story from the *Mahabharata* and Kalidasa had long been sublimated. Deep from sleep one night I found myself as Shakuntala asking the king "If your signet ring is not on my finger, then where is it?" The whole dance came to a climax at that moment: each figure springing into life as human beings puzzled at their own reaction to the situation, as perceived in the light of Destiny. When I created '*This Mahabharata*,' I sought parallels with everyday incidents happening all over the world. The realisation that minor incidents become magnified into an abandoning of all existing norms of behavior, the hurts to pride, ego, dignity, create acts of violence that echo through the ages. We are still not free from the bondage of past prejudices against caste, creed, and women and the so-called enemies. It emphasised the eternal qualities of peace and non-violence, and tried through understanding of past situations, the need for one universe, by universalising the old situations in modern concepts. Being a dance and a choreographer, every moment has meaning for me: while cherishing with deep love and reverence the technique needed to express my personal involvement in the world around me and to believe that I am a straight line, curving into infinite meaningful patterns.

Bharatanatyam

Rama vaidyanathan

Overview

by Rama Vaidyanathan

A dancer creates imagery in space with her body and soul capturing moments of life through movements, metaphors using the Angas as a vehicle to draw her own chitra. Of all the Angas mentioned in the Visnudharmottaram, Bhava and Lavanya are most crucial as they take her to the zenith of artistic creativity. For, it is the incorporation of these two Angas that transform her from a dancer to a creator. Complete internalisation of Bhava and Lavanya culminate to a point when the dancer and the dance become one — inseparable like the word and its meaning. Looking at Bhava Yojana separately leads us to this verse from Nadikeshwara's Abhinaya Darpana: Yates Hastastato Drishtiyarto Drishtistato Manaha, Yato Manastato Bhavo Yato Bhavastato Rasaha (Wherever the hand goes the glance goes, wherever the glance, there is the mind, wherever the mind is, Bhava is, and whenever there is Bhava, Rasa is created).This Shloka is best explained in the following example.

A dancer has to depict a woman pining for her beloved on a full-moon night. She moves her arm upwards with her hand in *Alapadma Hasta*. She looks at the moon created by her in space, with her mind making herself to believe that there is one there. Engulfed by the moonlight, her passion increases making her yearn for her lover. While depicting this, she becomes the *Nayika* completely oblivious of the world around her. For her, only the moon and her passion exist. It is only when she activates herself to feel this way, can she transfer this emotional experience to the audience. Her vibrations, laden with *Bhava*, get absorbed by the audience creating *rasa.* This is *Bhava Yojana*. It does not and cannot come to all and sundry. This is what makes this particular *Anga* so special. It is subjectivity and spontaneity makes it an aspect of dance which has to be inherently present in a dancer. Rather than acquire it through extraneous methods, she has to gradually cultivate it in her inner space. A dancer exposes herself completely as she dances. They say that the stage is the dancer's biggest mirror for it reflects her innermost thoughts and ideas. So when we take a close look at *Lavanya,* we realise that it is imperative for a dancer to be gracious and beautiful as a person, in order to manifest these qualities to the stage.

Lavanya encompasses several aspects of beauty in dance. It could be the way a dancer moves or smiles. It could be her taste in choice of music compositions, literature and *Aharya*. It could also be her charming countenance, her well-shaped body, long arms and expressive eyes. Most importantly, *Lavanya* is the aura around a dancer, the positive energy emanating from her which comes from the joy and satisfaction of creativity. *Lavanya* is all about balance, control and economy of movement: to express the most with the least, striking an optimum balance between the over-stated and the under-stated. A village belle is a picture of grace and control while she walks the tight rope in the village fair. A dancer too is constantly walking on a tight rope, making a thin line of distinction between *Lokadharmi* (extroverted and natural) and *Natyadharmi* (internalised and stylised). Only when she is able to walk this tight rope successfully can she be credited to have *Lavanya,* someone who is sensitised to the aesthetics. It is an inherent part of a dancer's persona which comes only after years of immersion in the arts.

Dance is a long journey from the physical to the spiritual, where the dancer's goal is to link her inner space with the outer space. Indian classical dance specially has tremendous formal richness and structural strength making the dancer sculpt space with movement. Her constant companions in this long journey would be *Bhava* and

Lavanya, for it is these two aspects of *Chitra* (picture) that bring that drastic transformation of a dancer from a mere human body to a creator. Her almost goddess-like picture is drawn not only because of her special *Aharya* but because of her communion with the metaphysical. Under the bright lights in all her finery, the dancer stands on the centre of the stage. With intense devotion, she folds her hands in *Anjali Hasta* to offer her obeisance to *Nataraja,* the Lord of Dance. At that moment, the space around her is sacred and the stillness in her body and soul make us to believe the presence of only herself and *Nataraja* – the *Jeevatma* and the *Parmatma*. This is the magic of *Bhava* and *Lavanya*.

The current scene is that dancers are capitalising on the fact that classical dance is a strong medium of communication. This is just as well because it is really high time we started using classical dance, — for more reasons than just to showcase the dance itself! As regards innovation, it is a tight-rope walk again, because one has to maintain a delicate balance between tradition and modernity. Classical dance by itself is so contemporary that we do not need a separate genre that can be dubbed: 'contemporary classical dance'!

CHANDRALEKHA: *The Undying Phenomenon*

Chandralekha, one of the greatest dancer-choreographers that India has produced, was often compared to another epochal dance-icon Isadora Duncan who blazed new trails in the Western world. Like Isadora, she took both physical and spiritual energy as her themes and revelled in them to the ultimate indissoluble point. Her life-long quest was: where does the body begin and end? If life is cyclic as she believed and if her mind was liberated from her body, she must have been thinking the same, — when her mortal body was consigned to holy flames on Sunday evening in Chennai, — having taken leave of this world in the midnight hours of 30-31 December 2006, after fighting a prolonged battle with cancer, eventually proved futile.

The life's journey of Chandan Patel of Baroda, who later named herself 'Chandralekha', was as full of intimations of bliss, as it was bristled with resistance from the Bharatanatyam dance fraternity as well as social opprobrium (she chose to live with her companion and critic Sadanand Menon). At 17, she had settled in Chennai. That was in 1946. Even while beginning her career in the early 1950's with *Arangetram*, when she was dancing the ritual dance *Mathura Nagarilo,* supposedly on the banks of the Yamuna, — she had the vision of the earth opening and swallowing up victims in a giant quake. This conflict between art and reality influenced all her work.

Chandralekha

The budding lawyer form Mumbai's Wilson College gave up her studies in favour of Bharatanatyam guided by the poet Harindranath Chattopadhyay and her celebrated guru Kancheevaram Ellappa Pillai, apart from deep influences of

Bala Saraswati, the legendary Devadasi dancer of Shringara fame and Rukmini Devi Arundale of Kalakshetra, an ardent votary of Bhakti. Interestingly, Chandralekha began rejecting the devotional elements of dance and chose to display body-oriented movements, choreographing passion, Bala-like.

With an abiding faith in feminism pervading her themes, Chandralekha's choreographic oeuvre was always in quest of the female and male energy, which she called 'celebrations of the human body'. She soon emerged as one of the most controversial Indian dancer-choreographers. Although termed variously as 'an iconoclastic maverick, a dancer who fused Bharatanatyam, yoga and Kerala's martial art of Kalari Payattu', she re-interpreted classical traditions in dance and developed a sequence of works, bearing her unique signature. *Angika* (1985) was a milestone in the Indian dance history, as it fused Bharatanatyam and Kalari Payattu. *Lilavati* (1989) was based on the algebraic puzzles of the 10th century mathematical text by Bhaskaracharya. *Prana* (1990) depicted movement of breath and the planets, in relation to yoga and dance. *Sri* (1991) was based on women's empowerment and enslavement; *Shakti* and Unity of *Prakriti-Purusha*— as culled from Harappan fertility images – were showcased in the House of World Cultures, Berlin in 1992.

Yantra: Dance Diagrammes (1994) was inspired by Adi Shankara's *Soundarya Lahar*i and showed how beauty was linked to an awareness of the body: both spiritually and sexually, and expressed through geometrical patterns, to signify female and male energies. *Mahakaal* (1995) went beyond linear notions of time, to explore the dance of timelessness, inner space and consciousness. Perhaps it was the most metaphysical of all her productions: with Chandralekha experimenting on intangible themes, such as, beginning of creation with cosmic sound, awareness of life and the eternal pulsation that continues between the cessation and genesis of the worlds. *Raga: In Search of Femininity* was founded on the erotica in the body and the search for femininity in the male, — by only exploring the primal essence of sensation. She was immediately hailed as the 'high priestess of the sensate'.

One cannot mistake a Chandralekha composition anywhere. Stark sets often set off by a single object: giant projection of a blinking eye; a geometrical figure; a Shiva lingam; or a scarlet rectangle representing the universal menstrual flow of creation. Her troupe of male and female dancers positioned themselves in intimate postures, — mistakenly called 'obscene' but for the masterly execution of each step and the subtle beauty of restricted erotica.

Loved, hated, admired, criticised — Chandralekha could be branded as a 'priestess of erotica', but not ignored or forgotten. Somewhere, those kohl-rimmed blue eyes, the bright vermilion mark on the forehead, the silver grey hairs, the deep lines of the face and the restrained power of the lithe body always caught one and lingered long after the fire was gone, as of now.

WONDERMENT PAR EXCELLENCE: *Malavika Sarukkai*

Malavika Sarukkai's dancing art has always been a visual treat. Backed by three decades of training in Bharatanatyam (tinged by a stint in the lyricism of Odissi, acquired from its best guru Kelubabu) and gifted with a lissome figure: the envy of the Chola bronze-masters, Malavika had presented vignettes of *Vision,* with a plural perception of spirituality, nature and abstract aesthetics: all through one's visual sense. Recently, she chose *Advuta – Vision of Wonder* as her theme. As everyone knows, the mysterious (or the wondrous) is one of the eight *Rasas* (sentiments), enumerated for the dramatic arts by the second-century *Natya Shastra* – covering the whole gamut from the erotic to the odious – to which the ninth 'peace' was added later. Asked, before the programme, on her choice of such an unusual sentiment, she points out, "I thought it offered enough potential for choreographic composition in my style." Pressed to comment whether this presages a new dance-oeuvre on all the *Nava Rasas,* she smiles, "Life is not always so linear. What happens in time to come, only future will tell!"

Malavika sarukkai

The choice of *Rasa* eventually turned out to be both right and enriching. First, *Mallari* emulates a temple procession — with nadaswarams — in *Raga Gambhira Nattai.* Laying emphasis on sculpture, the dancer strikes out friezes for elephant, mridangam, nadaswaram and the all-pervading wonderment at Shiva. The following *Mohana Krishnam* resurrects the 14th century verse of *Krihnakarnamritam* in a bouquet of *Ragas (Raga Malika)* and creates the spirit of miniature paintings. Images cascading down to the viewers are those of the swirling river Yamuna, the prancing peacocks, the entranced gopis and the lingering branches of the Tamal tree: in the enveloping ambience of overlaid dark clouds and dense woods with tender foliage. It is the mystique of the gopis' wondering adoration of the arrival of Krishna.

Krishnai Begani Baro, in *Raga Yemini Kalyani,* is indelibly associated with the legendary Bala Saraswati. Malavika created her filigree of *mudras* and footworks: to reveal Yashoda as angry, exasperated, diverted and, when the little Gopala eats mud, wild at the dirty act till she looks into the child's mouth to get wonderstruck at the whole cosmos sited within! The finale, *Samarpanam,* was a contrasting cameo of the romping, leaping, racing prankster of a Hanumana, who gazes in ultimate wonder when he finds his supreme lord and master: Rama. The refrain from Tulsidas' *Ramcharit Manas: Kauna Tuma Shyamala Shanta Sharira,* mellifouously sung by OS Arun in a mélange of *Ragas* like *Shivaranjini* and *Malayamarutham* was built into a delightful choreography.

Malavika summarises her attitude, "I've attempted them all: austerity and abundant passion; ecstasy and sensuality: always with an eye on communicativeness. I express what I see around me and feel about life: as observation, entertainment and performance. This evening's work is another frequency, another reality, like an *Anukeertanam* (short music-piece), — sharing with you something that can be alternately *Sattvik* (pure), quiet, energetic or humorous, taking due care that it is not debasing entertainment. It's part of one's choreographic journey!"

THE TAPESTRY OF BHARATANATYAM: *Alarmel Valli*

Alarmel Valli, among the most celebrated Bharatanatyam danseuses of this generation, has been a dancer's dancer. After a virtual blitzkrieg of prestigious international venues like Theatre de la Ville, Paris; Vienna International Festival, Austria; Festival of Normandy, France; and The Smithsonian Institute, Washington DC, — always in the company of an amazingly talented singer Savita Narasimhan – she charmed the cognoscenti at IIC paying homage to T.Mukhta, the formidable musician, who passed away last March. And, sure enough, Savita was there to accompany her in *Padams,* complex poetry and *Javalis,* exquisite love-songs, composed especially by Mukhta for dance.

Points out Alarmel, "For me, exciting aspects of her compositions lie in their infinite potential for personal interpretation of character, psychology and music, — particularly in the challenge of merging visual and aural experiences of the song. Not anecdotal and without linear narrative, these *Padams* and *Javalis* just capture a moment in time…" Elaborating on how Mukhta's musicality was intrinsic to Alarmel's personal style of dance, "Hers was unique music: profound, majestic, subtle, mellow and measured, — entirely different from vocal acrobatics or showy virtuoso flourishes." Further, "When I was a child, I saw many performances by the stalwart Balasaraswati who, for me, embodied the poetry of dance and music. I remember her once saying about *Abhinaya*: It can't be taught, but must flower on its own. Only when I studied music with Mukhta-Amma, I became aware of an entirely different dimension of *Abhinaya,* of hitherto hidden colours and shapes, — it was a revelation!"

Mukhta's music – with its nuances and curves, trills and pulses – was amply visualised by Alarmel in her choreographic oeuvre. The first was a *Padam* in *Raga Began,* narrating majestically the heroine's mindset: whom do I fear even if I'm entranced by him? The second was a *Javali* in flippant mood: How dares the one, who'd spent the night in my amorous embrace, taunt me from across the street in the dawn? The third was a *Kapodh-Raga Padam,* by Kshetraiya, about a sophisticated woman, unmoved by hero's ostentation, — set to 7 beats and taking off at quarter or half-beats, not at *Sams* (time-cycle's ends). The last one was *Kalyani-raga Javali* about a woman: startled, outraged and bewildered by the man in her life! The finale was a fascinating *Viruttam.* As Savita puts it, "It's a free-verse composition, riding on crests of a *Raga Malika: Sindhu Bhairavi, Poorvi Kalyani, Kapi, Verati, Neelambari* and *Madhyamavati."* Adds Alarmel, "I'm able to etch these ancient women's roles with my modern sensibility with ease and without compunction!"

The second evening saw Alarmel taking out some old nuggets like *Surya Ashtakam* built around an effulgent sun. The *Kamba Ramayana,* for instance, extolled the virtues of the sun as: *Divakaro Namostubhyam* and *Tubhyam Surya Pranamyaham,* in *raga Yemini Kalyani.* There were also verses from the 2000-year-old *Sangam* literature. Says Alarmel, "This was highly sophisticated secular poetry of the earliest times and the poet AK Ramanujam has transcribed them across centuries of culture with compelling immediacy. Two verses here are woven around *.ragas* like *Kannada,* describing a woman's plight like a fallen lemon as well as her fragrance like a jasmine-creeper in full bloom." The depiction was enchanting, but one did not comprehend why Alarmel had to splice such gems with a rather long-drawn, conventional *Pada-Varnam* in *raga Shankarabharanam.* The *Prema Shringara* was a departure from the general tenor of the evening, although Alarmel called the "passionate yearning" of the *nayika* as "both sensual and spiritual." How has Bharatanatyam changed over the last seven decades, after it was accepted in the late 1930's? Laughs Alarmel, "I can only trace it since the time I began dancing. Those were the days of great masters like Kittappa Pillai, Chokalingam Pillai, and my guru Subbaraya

Pillai (fortunately still alive, into his nineties) .and Meenakshi Sundaram Pillai's progeny. None of them was commercially-minded and set great stores by ideas. Money, in consequence, was put on the back burner. Again, there was no spoon-feeding. One had to learn from the vibes, from music and from what they didn't say! Also, they didn't hold back anything and I distinctly remember their explaining principles of choreography even when I was only15. Further, we didn't have technologies like computers, Internet, video-recorder and even cassette players, so that we had to rely solely upon our immediate learning and remain focussed on the lessons imparted. This was contrary to the 'crutches of technology' by helping to remember and recover later, rather than concentrate on what was taught. Creativity flowered effectively because I lacked technology in my youth!"

Continues she, "Today there are far more distractions. Children – and I've 30-32 learners — are pressurised under an education system that is flawed. I've known schools that often ran 7 days a week: repeatedly cycling study and examination. Where is the time 'to stand and stare', as Tennyson saw it? In my childhood years, our joint family would take time off annually for a month and a half for the hills of Kodaikanal, where uncles and aunts, nephews and nieces, would feed together on history and *Puranas*. We would brush up texts and stories in all three languages of Tamil, Sanskrit and English. Story-telling was kept at a premium as was playing games in the open fields, chasing butterflies and squirrels, and flying kites. There is hardly any open space today and big parks of Delhi are a rarity in Chennai!"

Concludes Alarmel thoughtfully, "Classical dance, as part of culture, does not permit instant gratification nor is it goal-oriented and result-specific. In an age of commercialisation today, it's more important to achieve quick results. On the contrary, humility – the awareness that you don't know it all – has disappeared. But yes, Bharatanatyam has grown, — with better use of space and even addition to vocabulary.

Like a banyan tree, it has spread out its branches. I'm a modern woman and my use of the style remains wholly contemporary to me!"

HERITAGE AND HISTORY OF BHAKTI: *Geeta Chandran*

Bhakti – offered to Krishna or Shiva or to multiple forms of Shakti as the ultimate divinity – has been a staple for countless centuries for Indian classical arts. But there's the nagging question: is worship of these godheads a post-*Mahabharata* phenomenon? The contrary viewpoint, remarkably well-argued in the award-winning work *Yuganta* by Irawati Karve, is that the epoch of the *Mahabharata* saw no gods; men and women were only occupied with their own actions and reaped consequences accordingly. Krishna and Arjuna were basically friends, and heroes and gurus like Bhishma and Drona did not demand any adulatory worship. Is it possible that after the utterly debilitating war of Kurukshetra, Krishna was raised to the pedestal of godhead in *Bhagavata* and *Harivamsa*, and the mediation of prayers and surrenders arose as an 'adjustment' in later epochs: worked out as 'compromise' of the human 'intellect'?

Geeta Chandran, the force behind *Jai Bharati* festival, is staunchly opposed to this idea, which needs debating out, according to her. "Bhakti in performing arts is the very fountain-head, the source of all our inspirations, without which the classical arts would become a circus", contends she. "Devoid of Bhakti, which is part of our heritage and history, our forms do not amount to anything. Ours are dedicated arts to propitiate the gods, much like the prayers proffered in *Yajnas*. The venerable saint poets, over the ages, have bequeathed us beautiful literature threading through spirituality and Bhakti: full of expressive imagery and deep philosophy. In our programme, we've attempted – through *Saguna* Bhakti for Krishna — to visualise some of those images in our individual styles."

Geeta Chandran

Leela Sampson

Jai Bharati, billed as 'unique voyage in classical dance through the prism of Bhakti', is a robust vindication of Geeta's argument. Eight well-known dancers go even a step further: they use verses not normally germane to their six styles. The curtain-raiser is with all the dancers performing together to an exquisite chant: *Namo Nalini Netraye, Benu Vadya Vinodin:* sung by Madhup Mudgal who orchestrated memorably the music for the programme. The dancers' finishing freezes: as mythical characters of Prahlad, Vibhisana, Gajendra (of Gajendra-Moksha legend), Panchali, Ahalya and Dhruva: were superb.

Then comes the individual odes to Krishna. Singhajit Singh and Charu Sija Mathur execute, in Manipuri, a Meera Bhajan: *Ko Kahiyo Re Prabhu Awan-ki Mana Bhao:* in *Raga Yaman.* Shovana Narayan renders Kathak to an unlikely Purandara Dasa Kriti in *Raga Kapi: Jagat Uddharate:* steeped in *Vatsalya rasa.* Mohiniyattam by Bharati Shivaji uses the verse of poetess Andaal: *Varana Mayivar:* in *Raga Malika.* Geeta's own Bharatanatyam, to a *Shuddha Sarang* piece by Ras Khan: *Prem Ayoni Shri Radhika, Prem Varana Nanda Nanda:* is brilliant in *Anga Shuddhi* and *Kala Pramanam.* Odissi by Madhavi Mudgal uses the lilting *Vasant Vahar* to pine away with: *Bin Gopala:* by Surdas. The sixth style is Kuchipudi by the duo Jaya Rama Rao and Vanashree, performed to two *Ashtapadis* by Jayadeva: *Ya Hi Madhava* in *Ragas Bibhas* and *Jogiya,* and *Priye Charushile* in *raga Bhopali:* to make a dance-drama minuet. The finale is again with all the dancers choreographing together, in *Raga Malika,* Vallavacharya's *Madhura Ashtakam,* the most famous of all the Ashtachhap poetry.

"In today's increasingly cynical world, where the crass is being eagerly embraced and the subtle is shunned for the obvious and the garish, ours is an effort to reiterate the values and culture that have given our culture its edge," avers Geeta. Against the magnificent backdrop of the white filigree-laced Vrindavan temple façade, made of banana fibre, the evening was an ethereal experience!

VIGNETTES OF FEMININISM: *Urmila Sathyanarayana*

It was a 'hop, step and jump' for classical Bharatanatyam. In *Stree Shakti: A Thematic Presentation in Praise of Womanhood,* the Chennai-based veteran danseuse Urmila Sathyanarayana hopped into the mythological arena in her *Mathe Daru,* breathed deeply to collect her step and then – much like an adroit sportswoman – took a huge jump to her prime goal, *Woman: Past, Present, Future.* It was, in other words, a great performance.

To depict the 'past', Urmila begins with an ode to the 'Shubhankari' (benevolent) goddess Meenakshi, the legendary consort of Shiva Sundareswara and the mother of Ganesha Vinayaka and Karthikeya Murugan. This was femininity par excellence, steeped

Urmila Satyanarayanan

choreographically in the tradition of Dandayudhapani Pillai, KJ Sarasa and the indomitable Kalanidhi Narayanan. Another mythological tribute follows to the mother goddess, 'Bhayankari' (malevolent) this time, the fierce Chamundeswari: who would slay the lecherous womaniser-demons Chanda and Munda, and restore balance in an erotica-obsessed world.

This attitude to a balanced approach — between the virtuous and the vicious – informed her major work on womanhood. Elaborates Urmila; "The poetic support was from the academician VV Subramaniam, fondly called 'Va Ve Su' in the Tamil literary circle. The concept was mine and we worked together to visualise the thoughts." The 'past' is in the garb of myths again: the courageous Savitri, who challenges Yama, the fierce god of death; and the ever-pliable Nalayini, who sacrifices her self-respect to carry physically a sick husband to the bed-chamber of a harlot. It was also part history: the Queen of Jhansi who fights the brave battle against the British. At the other historical pole is the child-bride and sati of a vile society. Starting with the theme *Raga Ahir Bhairon, Ragas* for the 'past' are resplendently drawn: *Valagi, Karaharapriya, Simhendra Madhyamam, Sumani Ranjini* and *Hamsanadam.*

The 'present' too comes at two levels. On one hand, the woman is the multinational technocrat as well as both caring mother and loving wife on the home front, who has to tackle the influx of sudden guests and bear the brunt. At the other plane, she is the wretched housemaid, who nourishes hungry children, remains ever pregnant and supports a drunken husband, to get beaten in the process by the latter. The missing balance is explored, — now through Carnatic folk-tunes. The 'future' is probably the glorious morning to come, where woman finally balances compassion with strength and hones both knowledge and independence with an equally poised life. The music takes on a strident Western colour, — with a touch of *Raga Des.*

"I was asked to do the theme by a Chennai organisation and had the International Woman's day on 8 March in mind. I wanted to present the idea in black and white: with a clash between virtue and vice in past and present, but hold out hope for a bright and blameless future. Certainly it couldn't be through orthodox Bharatanatyam. I'd to invent a choreographic style within the frame of my learnt skills and acquired techniques, — and then jell with the theme by going much beyond!"

GEMS OF BHARATANATYAM FROM THE SOUTH: *Roja Kannan*

When the veteran guru of Bharatanatyam, Adyar Lakshmanan of Chennai brought his ace disciple Roja Kannan to perform in Capital, it was one of the guru's rare appearances in the north. Lakshmanan is a star protégé of Rukmini Devi, and was literally reared up by her at the prestigious Kalakshtera. And there upon hangs a tale. Guru Adyar Lakshmanan has been a carrier of the legacy of Kalakshetra in its pristine purity. This legacy is born of the tutelage there of gurus like Meenakshi Sundaram Pillai and comes from the hoary Tanjavoor school that follows rigorous discipline of limbs and body-movements, with clear *Mudras* and extensions. This is quite distinct from the Vazhuvoor School: the other approach to less rigid lines and movements, as taught by gurus like Kitappa Pillai of yore. As a worthy recipient of the Kalakshetra legacy, Roja displayed all the versatility of her heritage: right from the word 'go'.

She began with a *Pushpanjali* (flower offering), based on Shivastuti, a chant to Shiva, followed by a *Nandi Shloka* (ode to Nandi, Shiva's carrier). In these items, she demonstrated the Shaivaite rites of passage. Although there is an accepted dichotomy among the rituals owing to Shiva and those to Vishnu, the Shaivaites are generally less rigid in following them, in contrast to the practice adhered to by Vaishnavites. What followed was an illuminating *Varnam*: the core-piece of Bharatanatyam: using both *Nritta*, the purely gesture-dance and *Nritya*, the other kind of dance that interprets music. This elaborate item was based on a garland of multiple *Ragas* and interpreted a tribute to Brihadishwara Shiva, the Lord of dance, — composed by the Tanjavoor quartet. And thereupon hangs yet another tale.

The four brothers – Chinnaiya, Ponnaiya, Shivanandan and Vadivelu – were the gifted court dancers, belonging to the mid-19th century, who regaled the king of Tanjavoor. The brothers used to teach the *devadasis* and evolved a *Margam* to be followed by every dancer: *Alarippu* (invocation), *Jatiswaram* (dance with rhythmic mnemonics), *Shabdam* (dance based on musical notes), *Varnam* (complete dance comprising both abstraction and literary interpretation), *Padam* (dance with lyrical music), *Javali* (dance with erotic poetry) and *Tillana* (fast rhythmic dance in conclusion). It goes to the redounding credit of the Tanjavoor quartet that this *Margam* has passed the test of time and is still followed in all traditional repertoires of Bharatanatyam.

Roja proved her mettle by continuing her programme with two diametrically opposite *Padams*: the first, a traditional Swathi Thirunal composition in Malayalam; and the second, a Tamil piece by the 20th century poet Subramania Bharathi: covering two contrary aspects of a woman! The first lyric bore a lamentation of the *Virohotkanthita Nayika* (the forlorn heroine): *I have nowhere to go and none besides him, why has he forgotten me?* The second composition was the clarion call of a *Khandita Nayika* (enraged heroine): *I'm not going to cry over a man who has jilted me, let him intimate what his intentions are and whether he proposes to come or not...* This indeed is Subramania's modern woman, in thought and deed, who wants to map out her own life! The finale was a *Tillana* in *Raga Hindalam* bringing the evening to a fitting end.

WHERE HERITAGES MEET: *Chitra Chandrasekhar Dasararathy*

In his famous book *Myths to Live By*, Joseph Campbell wrote, "Recognition of morality and the requirement to transcend it is the first great impulse to mythology. And along with this, there runs another realisation, namely, that the social group, — into which the individual has been born, which nourishes and protects him, and which he must himself help to nourish and protect, — was flourishing long before his own birth and will remain when he is gone."

One mythology, held in common in the heritage of Egypt, Greece and India, is the concept of supreme feminine power at the genesis of all creativity. In Egypt, she is *Hathor* – whose mammoth figures and seated postures dominant in bass-relief on the inside rock-face of the tombs – the goddess of fertility and agriculture, revelry and joy. She is the daughter of the sun, Ra and commands the floodwaters of the Nile. Every ancient Pharaoh had to claim divinity by drinking her milk. In Greece, she is Aphrodite, the goddess of fertility, beauty and sexual love. Daughter of Zeus, she is born into foams, to step ashore from a scallop shell, to be judged by Paris as the most beautiful of the goddesses and to become the root cause of the Trojan War. In India, she is the primal *Devi*, the Mother Goddess, who is *Shakti* to Shiva, the creative energy of *Prakriti* to the passive *Purusha*. "Seven *Hathors* in Egyptian mythology come to bless a child, just as in our mythology, there are *Sapta Matrika* (like *Brahmani, Vaishnavi, Aindreyee, Kaumari* and others), extolled in *Devi Mahatman*, who comprise together the feminine energy of the cosmic gods," says the young Bharatanatyam dancer Chitra Chandrasekhar Dasarathy.

Chitra presents *Sama Veda: Hathor and I,* as an ode to the Egyptian heritage, in Bharatanatyam style. It was a heroic figuration where she appeared imbued with the spirit of *Hathor* who, as she explains, "presides over the skies. At her festival, the earth is flooded with joy and the sky rejoices with music and dance." Chitra brought her profound wonderment and awe in the chiselled *adavus*, followed by a communion with *Hathor* where the great goddess – "Who is everywhere, on the walls of the temples and in the lives of those who built these temples" – is resplendent in her golden glory. Awakened from her languorous sleep, *Hathor* enters Chitra's world of the Indian heritage: the legacy of the Kabir bhajan: *Guru Govind Dou Khade*; the symbolic Tamil *Padam: Netru Varen Enru* that presents a woman awaiting her lover; the first verse from Kalidasa's *Ritu Samharam* describing the blissful state of togetherness; and the Surdas lyric: *Yasoda Hari Palne* on the sacred bonds between the mother and the child. She concludes with her own dance rendering on Nazrul Islam who wishes to sculpt a new image of Krishna, if only given the right granite (*Ami Nutan Kore Godbo Thakur*).

Chitra's very originality of the idea of confrontation of civilisations – Egyptian and India – made her creativity run away with her enthusiasm. What were direly needed were some visuals on *Hathor* and her magnificent presence in the temples, pyramids and pillared halls. This could be followed by an animated narration (and not a long reading from a prepared text that put many in the audience to sleep) and a vivid re-creation of *Hathor*'s seated figures and standing postures vis-à-vis the well-depicted Bharatanatyam stances. The accompanying *Sahitya* could also be carefully tuned to the theme on hand. This is certainly not to detract from the very novel experiment to broaden the classical dance-form's horizons that Chitra attempted. All kudos to her for this, with a fresh mind daring into uncharted territories: enriching us in the process.

LORD OF COSMIC DANCE: *Santosh Nair, Shantnu Chakraborty*

The Hindu pantheon is redolent with the dancing anklets of its principal gods: *Nataraja* Shiva and *Natawar* Krishna, quite unlike the Greek mythology where none of the towering divinities like Zeus, Venus, Jupiter or Athena are ever associated with performing arts. Music and dance are ubiquitous in Indian mythology, — with, now, Saraswati playing veena, Brahma cymbals, Vishnu flute, Shiva *dambaru,* Nandi mridangam, alongside the dancing Ganesha at the head of the *ganas* (Shiva'a minions) and the singing sage Narada. Their distant Westen cousins in high heavens are the nine Greek muses, originally the daughters of Zeus, made later the presiding deities of the arts: with only Terpsichore personifying choral dance and song! Interestingly, even Buddhism's Tantrik form of *Vajrayana* has gods and goddesses celebrated in *Charya Nritya*: the esoteric dance preserved in Nepal's reclusive monasteries.

Santnu Chakraborty

In the world of dance where Shiva has been a favourite god depicted by every female danseuse, it was a refreshing change to watch two male dancers presenting Shiva in his effulgent beauty on two successive evenings: Santosh Nair as *Nataraj –The Lord of Dance* and Shantnu Chakraborty as *Shambho Mahadeva.*

Out of the two, *Nataraj* was premiered earlier and the production – with nearly a score of youthful dancers from 'Sadhya' — comes packaged in a more resplendent form and with ethereal music. In the performance, Shiva is first the timeless and space less lord of the universe, then transforming himself to the supreme creator of cosmos in a blinding plurality. He then comes, with consort Shakti, as ideal lover-duo, with both spirit and substance residing in oneness. Lastly, Shiva is seen as destroyer of darkness, tearing asunder illusory bonds of the fleeting world, where his dance leads to salvation.

Says Santosh, "Shiva's personality, as a male, complements my own masculinity, since I've always visualised him as a Yogi, a guru. In my own learning of Chhau, I found Shiva central to my own entity!" Responding to the point why he depicted multiple Shiva-s and multiple Shakti-s that resembled *Maha Raas,* where every Gopi had her personal Krishna, explains Santosh, "To me, it's a reflection of man-woman coupling that is inspired by Shiva-Shakti conjugality." And on destruction of evil, "It's Shiva removing negative energy and letting loose positive energy. At the end, doesn't he suck away the world's poison and become *Nilakantha* (blue-throated god)?" Santosh's break-neck tempo in choreography perhaps needs more punctuation by meaningful pauses, while utilising the potential of many *Tandavas* in Chhau-based choreography, especially *Gauri-Tandava* in Shiva-Shakti duality. Santosh agrees in toto!

Shambho Mahadeva, in contrast, is out-and-out traditional. Shantnu followed guru V. Krishnamurthy's Pandannalur choreography to portray a virile Shiva through eclectic verses in Sanskrit and Tamil. *Shiva Panchakshara Stotra* by Shamkara: *Nagendra Haraya Trilochanaya, Bhasmanga Ragaya Maheshwaraya....:* is a lilting lyric, followed by Dayananda Saraswati's rousing composition: *Bho-Shambho Shiva Shambho Swayam Bho...* in *Raga Revathi.* A beautiful *Ananda Tandava* is rendered tuned to Kalyani Sundaram Pillai's *Thiru Chitra Ambalam* in *raga Kalyani,* with a *Tillana* in *Raga Hindolam* as the finale.

Ananda Shankar Jayant

Elaborates Shantnu on the many subtleties he introduced within the traditional framework, "I depicted *Nirguna-Saguna* aspects — with and without attributes — in the first verse, while taking it through the process of awakening *Kundalini* (inner Shakti) from toe through navel, shoulder and face, to ultimately head. Dayananda's was a prayerful exaltation of the infinite expanse of the phallic symbol, unfathomed by the gods, whereas both *Ananda Tandava* and *Tillana* were joyful celebrations of the lord." Santana's own dance was captivating, but the same could not be said of his four disciples: still away from having achieved *Anga Shuddhi* (tuned bodylines)!

BESEECHING THE BENIGN BUDDHA: *Ananda Shankar Jayant*

Sarve Pratyante Dandeshu sarvesham Jeevitam Priyam / Atmanam Upamam Kritya Na Hantaye Na Ghataye — Dharmapada (Buddhist scripture)

When the compassionate prince Siddhartha rebuked his hunter-cousin Devadutta who had just brought down a flying swan to the ground, he had voiced only a universal truth: nobody wants to be punished as life is dear to all of us; if we compare our soul as an analogy, we will learn not to hurt or kill others. Shankaranada Kalakshetra from Hyderabad depicts this and many other morals in their dance-drama *Buddham Sharanam Gacchami*, directed by the veteran dancer Ananda Shankar Jayant.

Buddham... is a delightful delineation of the life and philosophy of the Buddha through a string of legends: covering king Shuddhodhana's court; queen Maya's dream; birth of the prince Siddhartha in the Lumbini gardens; the youthful prince learning martial arts and horse-riding; the encounter with Devadutta; the marriage with Yashodhara and birth of Rahul; the revealing chariot-journey to witness old age, disease, death and spiritual bliss; the renunciation of palace-life; the temptations by Mara and his daughters; the enlightment under the Bodhi tree; and the preaching of eight-fold paths and four truths. Presented in the well-known Kalakshetra style, the eleven dancers used Bharatanatyam in traditional costumes alongside crowns and *lahengas*.

"I belong to the Kalakshetra genre, having learnt there from 1973-79," declares Ananda. "My training and performance covered all the twenty-five episodes of the *Ramayana* so ably staged by Rukmini Devi, besides ballets like *Meenakshi Vijayam, Damayanti Swayamvaram* and *Kumara Sambhavam*, especially as Rati in the latter. My institution at Hyderabad is a result of my deputation to that state, from my parent cadre in the Indian Railway Traffic Service. Despite my career concerns, dance continues to be my life-breath!"

Two fascinating tales from the Buddhist lore enrich *Buddham*.... First is Angulimala, the dreaded brigand who promises a garland of 100 severed human heads to his master. After the 99 killings are over, it is the Buddha's turn, but there is little success. Instead, the robber is enchanted by the sermons and adopts his path. In the second story from *Saundarya Anandan* by Ashwaghosh, Siddhartha's sibling Nanda is madly in love with consort Sundari and cannot brook a moment's separation. Meanwhile, the mendicant Buddha comes to seek alms and, while ignored first, Nanda comes later with offerings. The Buddha's bowl falls in his palms and Nanda is now transfixed. After Sundari's angry remonstration, the Buddha teaches the couple higher truths of life.

A scene from "Shodashopocharam"

On the choice of Sanskrit as her script language, Ananda avers, "I'm comfortable in Sanskrit and have used the original script. When one is talking about *Margani Ashtami Shreshtham*..., the flavour of the Buddhist teachings is best conveyed through the basic text in Pali. I've used the Sanskrit variation: to bring out the resplendence of the language.'

Smt. Narmada

SIXTEEN RITES, EIGHT REGINA:

Uma Anantani

Rituals have been celebrated in Indian classical music in a myriad ways. In the south, the eighteenth-century saint-poet Thyagaraja wrote his famous *Kritis* for rituals: as simple, emotional outpourings of a *Bhakta*, praying to his Lord. Collectively, these were *Utsava Sampradaya Kritis* and formed part of *Divyanama Sankirtana*. This *Sankirtana* was a common part of *Bhakti* movement and could be sung for twelve to fourteen hours in a nightlong worship, — beginning from the *Nama-Japa* in the evening, through the *Kritis* with *Prana-Pratistha* of idol, and ending with distribution of *prasad* in the early morning. The *Kritis* alone could be sung as special offerings in the daily worship-rituals: from early morning waking up of Rama, to putting him back to bed at night.

The other eighteenth century saint-poet Muthuswamy Dikshitar was an ardent devotee of Devi, especially of Kamalamba at Thiruvayoor. His musical compositions, known as *Sahasra Nama Archana*, had architectonic *Kritis* very akin to *Tantrik* drawings. *Shri Chakra* is one such quintessential part of *Tantrik* faith – where there are nine crossings from periphery to the centre – worshipping a specific deity at each crossing. These *Naba Abharanas* are released one by one in

Dikshitar's nine *Kritis*, to reach Lalitamba at the culmination point, — in his *Lalita Sahasra Nama*. The most interesting point to note is that both Thyagaraja's and Dikshitar's *Kritis* are still part of the daily rituals in the South.

'Rasadhwani' presented the Bharatanatyam dance-drama *Shodashopocharam*, based on sixteen temple rituals, from Ahmedabad. Outlining her choreography, the director Uma Anantani explains, "In the Shri Nathji temples, we too have rituals celebrated in music. Our Haveli Sangeet, which is a precursor of classical music, has many passages culled from *Vishnu Dharmottar Purana*. Pt. Jasraj's Mewati *gharana,* in fact, is a direct descendent of Haveli music." The sixteen rituals in *Shodasha* begin with *Suprabhatam* (morning chants), *Snana* (bath), *Vastradana* (clothes-offering), *Pushpa Shringara* (flower decoration), *Chandan Lepan* (sandalwood adornment), *Hindol Sthapan* (swing placement), *Naivedya* (food offering), and so on, — on to *saundarya kriti* (adoration of beauty), *Mangal Arati* (evening prayers*), Shayan Kaksha Nimantran* (invitation to the bed) and, finally, lullaby. All these come wonderfully alive in the dance-compositions: beginning with meditations at dawn and culminating into trance-movements as the night spread. The music appropriately captures the rhythm and melody of the original hymns to Narayana as the presiding deity, symbolically placed in the backstage.

Another heritage of Gujarat is some 500-and-odd poems by the saint-poet Narsinh Mehta, perhaps the best known of which is *Vaishnava Janato*... that so much inspired Mahatma Gandhi. Belonging to the 16th century, Narsinh's poetic oeuvre has always been cherished for their supreme *Bhakti* element and triggered imagination of many singers, composers, actors and dancers in Gujarat. "The inner and outer beauty of the female soul, as visualised by Narsinh, can be reflected through the physical, mental and spiritual conditions and the various moods presented as *Ashta Nayikas,*" contends Uma. "Each dancer as a *Nayika* is associated with a *Nayak*, even as they dance together in a musically well-crafted item." Through an imaginative choreography, the dancers created many solo, duet and group compositions.

Rasaraja Krishna is the other item based on *Shrimad Bhagavat*. Again, *Uttama, Madhyama* and *Adhama* personae were created around *Navarasa* of *Natya Shastra*. Conceived on a single *Shloka*, where Krishna is battling Kamsa amidst conflicting emotions all around, the *rasas* were played out most innovatively. Uma deserves kudos for pulling off some captivating dance compositions with a refreshingly young troupe.

COALESCING CAREER & CHOREOGRAPHY: *Savitri Ramaiah, Padmini Sirish, AR Sridhar*

A time was when the Bharatanatyam Guru KP Kittappa Pillai or the Odissi doyen Kelucharan Mohapatra or the Kuchipudi and Kathak maestros Vempat Chinna Satyam and Birju Maharaj would train

AR Sridhar

gifted disciples to their heart's content and, in turn, the finished student would have the satisfaction of making dance a life-time vocation. Not any longer. In the competitive age of professional careers luring the youth – howsoever honed the dance-talent is – into divergent, lucrative domains with hardly any time to spare, the dancing passion can really recede into background. Right? Wrong again.

Savitri Ramaiah, an MD, specialised in Preventive Medicine. After running a highly informative 'Health Digest' for five years, she is currently engaged in capacity building in reproductive child health and HIV/AIDS for training NGOs and doctors. She also learnt Bharatanatyam from Guru Smt. Narmada, the first student of Kittappa Pillai and is an accomplished dancer. "My career is not divided", asserts Savitri. "Having two vocations was a dream come true. Learning dance and choreography has proved indeed so relaxing that it prevents me from burning out!"

Padmini Sirish from Bangalore, of the same lineage as Savitri's, gave recently her maiden performance in the Capital. She had her *Arangetram* (first public performance) at the unbelievable age of 7 ½ and, now at 28, she regaled the audience with a Varnam woven in *Ashtaraga-Malika*: *Todi, Shankaravaranam*, *Pantuvarali, Attana, Kalyani, Vasantha, Mukhari* and *Bhairavi*. Her Purandara Dasa composition of Devarnama was in *Raga Yemani Kalyani*: depicting what a delightful prankster little Krishna was in hiding away Yashoda's churning stick! The finale was a Tillana, composed by the famed mridanga-player TV Gopalakrishnan with mathematical precision, in a wonderful *Raga Rathipathi*. Now on the flip side: Padmini, student of life sciences, is on her doctoral programme in Cellular and Molecular Biology at the California State University in Davis for the last four years." I received early acclaim in dance and knew that dance would be my principal preoccupation, but I liked biology, too", confesses Padmini. "I find dance ever so relaxing and don't believe in not finding time for my practice. I plan to become eventually a dance-teacher, so that there will be no conflict."

AR Sridhar, who had danced both solo and duet with Pratibha Prahlad in Bharatanatyam, is a practising physician in Bangalore. He did a diploma in Industrial Health as well. Both the medicine and dance worlds have gained by his profession and passion. Dr Kamala Reddy has been a gifted student of Vempati Chinna Satyam in Kuchipudi, but studied in a medical school. There is another child prodigy, Srinidhi Rasngarajan who, too, was a medical school product. She practises her vocation and also dances abroad where she is settled. The other noted dancer, and disciple of Maharaj-ji, is Shovana Narayan in Kathak, a senior bureaucrat in Indian Audit & Accounts Service. Adds Madhavi Mudgal, Kelu Babu's foremost disciple, "R Parvathi, a product of medical school, has been my student, who has not given up Odissi, while practising abroad."

Can any one vocation tilt the balance over the other? Responds Savitri, "You need support for keeping up your dance career. Not getting funds and platforms can lead to disillusionment. One does have to strive. Fortunately, as a consultant, I can apportion time. Shovana possibly apportions time from her evenings and weekends. It's the most important thing not to give up!"

BARODA'S BECKONNING BHARATANATYAM:
Parul Shah

Baroda today is a citadel of Bharatanatyam where almost every girl seeks to learn the classical form. But how does Gujarat, especially Baroda, lures and nurtures the style imported all the way from the Tamil shores? The fascinating story goes back to 1880 when Sayaji II, the Gaekwad of Baroda, married Chimana Bai of Tanjavoor and received two devadasis as bride's maids along with a group of musicians The royal court continued its liberal patronage to the arts spanning 1875-1950 – with stalwarts like Pandit Omkar Nath Thakur and Ustad Faiyaz Khan, among others, finding niche in the durbar. Another group of classical dancers followed with musicians in the 1920's. The chain bloomed over the years and common men got exposed to the style: while going to the court or during many cultural celebrations.

Adds Parul Shah, whose group 'Anjali Memorial Committee' from Baroda recently presented: *From Tradition to Contemporary*. "The MS University of Baroda also played a key-role. After Mohan Khokar relinquished the charge of departmental head in dance, Anjali Merh took over. She was among the first batch of students, from 1939, under Rukmini Arundale at Kalakshetra and, as a gifted Gujarati dancer, worked till late 1950s, introducing education in classical performance with great élan. An almost Baroda *Gharana* in Bharatanatyam has grown now!"

The distinctive heritage was evident when Pushpanjali with Khanda Jati (5-beats) in *Raga Natai* was performed, followed by 7-beat Jatiswaram in *Raga Malika* (garland). Besides the unusual beats, the traditional choreography reflected well-honed movements and carved out space in geometric patterns with great ingenuity. Next was the famous Keertanam in *Raga Arabhi*: *Ananda Natam Adunar:* by Dr. Ami Pandya, having researched on Adavus into Abhinaya. Parul, transited to the contemporary idiom by expatiating on a Gujarati Padam in *Yaman*: How do I know what he finds in me, in the spirit of Swadhina Bhartika Nayika, and eight dancers (mostly university-students) collaborated on the famous Narsinh Mehta Bhajan: *Vaishnavajana To Tene Re Kahiye*. Laughs Parul, "In the 'Gandhigiri' years, I'm conveying Gandhi's message in Bharatanatyam, — with costumes in striking white and saffron, touched off by blue. Basically, we use Gujarati, in which my dancers think and speak. While they do analyse Tamil or Telugu pieces threadbare, Gujarati comes naturally to them for dance-expressions. Indeed, we've complete Bharatanatyam *Margam* (repertoire) in Gujarati!"

Expressions by Parul interpreted a breath-taking contemporary troika: Jagjit Singh's ghazal: *Tum Jetna Muskara Rahe Ho*, Bhupen Hazarika's rendering: *Vistaar Hai Apaar* from Paul Robeson's 'Ole Man River' and children's doggerel: *Ma, Suna Do Mujhe Woh Kahani*. The finale was an elaborate take on our earth: birth of planets; beginning of life from water to plants, animals and humans: exuberance of living creatures like butterflies; hunting and the hunted; defoliation and destruction: and greed versus compassion. While choreography was scintillating, the theme was too ambitious.

The last word is Parul's, "There has also been a two-way traffic, — with Baroda's Chandan Patel becoming 'Chandralekha' in Tamil Nadu and immensely contributing to the national and international Bharatanatyam scenario. Her demise on 30 December is an irreparable loss!"

MOOD DANCE, INSTANT VERSE: *Kanaka Srinivasan*

Kanaka Srinivasan

Bharatanatyam has reached its 'critical mass' at long last, which Kathak has been showing off all along. Birju Maharaj, for instance, would suddenly get up – as happened in the last Kalashram festival – with his brand new 'Hori' poem and bashful Saswati Sen would begin splendid improvisation at Maharaj-ji's prompting. Or Uma Sharma, for that matter, would display *Abhinaya* impromptu to Jwala Prasad's soulful

Ghazal. This is what *Upaj* (creative improvisation) is in Kathak: a delectable fare usually present in some *Jugalbandi* or the other among the dancer-singer-percussionist trio. But it is certainly a 'no-no' in the classical Bharatanatyam (or Mohiniyattam or Kuchipudi) where only set pieces of repertoire are executed in both abstract and interpretative dance on stage. Departing from the pre-structured format would definitely be a sacrilege!

And here comes the ace danseuse Kanaka Srinivasan, a prize disciple of Vazhuvoor Ramiah Pillai and a leading exponent of his style, who breaks all mental barriers and begins improvising to pure verses: three Tamil ones by the aesthete M Varadarajan, three Hindi ones by the noted litterateur-bureaucrat Ashok Vajpeyi and three Tamil ones by the budding Chennai poetess Kanimozhi (daughter of Karunanidhi). Here are Kanaka's words, "I've danced to only one of them, by Varadarajan, earlier. But the other eight were brand new and musically they were totally virgin territory! OS Arum, the gifted composer, arrived the previous day and we passed him the poems of Varadarajan and Vajpeyi. Kanimozhi brought her musings only on the performance-day and had to be hastily changed, being too abstract. Luckily, they were *terra cognita* to me, being Tamil, to which I could emote directly on stage!" This is a far cry from emoting to set stanzas, lines, phrases and words: as done in conventional Bharatanatyam!

Woh Ati Hai / To Lagta Hai Ho Rahi Hai Subah — / Ati hai Phulon Me Silsilahat, / Pattiyon Me Kanpkanpahat, / Chidiyon Me Chahchahahat..., penned Vajpeyi. Arun set it to *Raga Mishra Behag*, in the mood of Ghazal. The second Hindi offering: *Vachan Dekar Bhi Nahin Ata Priya / Prateeksha Ke Anant Ke Vrint Par / Khile Woh Kalee Sochtee Hai? Yeh Mare Vasant Mein Patjhar Kyun Lag Raha Hai*... that became *Raga Bhupalam*, in the *Madhyama Shruti by a* shift of scale. Vajpeyi's last poem was: *Usne Apne Prem ke Liye Jagah Banayee / Buharkar Alag Kar Diya Taraon Ko / Surya -Chandrama Ko Rakh Diya Ek Taraf,* which was transmuted to an explosive *Yemini-Kalyani* in Arun's voice. Avers Vajpeyi; "I blend simplicity of Hindi diction with the grandeur of classical imagery!" Says Arun, "It is the regard to poetic language that makes me decide the *Raga* and its exposition. While for Kanimozhi's first piece: *I got tired searching for myself till the moon rose, — I'm not the same woman any more, but one who has changed...,* I used the pensive *Raga Megh.* But for her second poem: *My Grandmother told me there would be insects in the dark room...:* which spoke first of obedience and then of defiance, I used a lullaby-kind *Behag* changing to a more spirited melody. Her third poem: *The bee left behind footprints on the fallen pollen...* I was undecided until my arrival on the proscenium and took advice form a *Rasika* for improvising in *raga Des* and catch the *Sthayee Bhava* (enduring emotion)." Adds Kanimozhi from Chennai, "I had visualised three women: besotted in love but disappointed, tired of social pleasure and engaged in vigorous action."

While the above were mood music in consonance with poetic spirits, Varadarajan's were mainly sparks of divinity, — on the slaying of Ganapati by her irate father Shiva; on the comparison between Kartikeya (or Kandappa), Tamil Nadu's dear protector and Krishna of Kerala's Guruvayur Temple; and on a picaresque description of the oddball Shiva who sports awkward tastes and testimonials. Arun's spirited tunes waxed and waned accordingly: from *Ragas Hamsanandi* to *Dhurmabati* to finally *Raga Malika.* Through this entire mood: Vajpeyi's abstraction and imagery, Kanimozh's quest for the feminine reality and Varadarajan's divine attributes: it was Kanaka's tentativeness and temerity that held sway; ushering in Bharatanatyam's new genre of 'mood dance' in step with' mood music'!

SUBRMANIA BHARATI AND SHIVA: FUELLING FIRE

Saroja Vaidyanathan

Chinnaswamy Sub mania Bharati (1882-1921) was a phenomenon of his time. Poet, prose-writer, journalist and patriot, he blazed

Saroja Vaidyanathan

a new trail in every domain and evinced a range of inspiration, which was amazingly vast, considering the briefness of his life span. His poems dwelt upon: patriotism and national regeneration; hymns to the deities of Indian pantheon; philosophy imbibing the thoughts of *Upanishads;* elements of nature; ecstatic outpourings on *Shakti*; romantic songs on Krishna; and narrative poetry. But, above all, he was the fiery poet of the masses in furthering the public causes and giving voice to the anguish of the Tamil multitude and their longings for a better future. Indeed, he dreamt many dreams for removing cobwebs of prejudices and for India's social regeneration much of which remain still unfulfilled!

'Ganesha Natyalaya' presented a thematic programme on *Women Empowerment and Patriotism*, based on Bharati's poems, by Saroja Vaidyanathan and her talented troupe. This was an elaboration of her earlier work on Bharati's patriotic songs produced in 1986 and did full justice to the still burning issues of: women's liberation; adoration of the youth; women's slave-labour in the Fiji Island; nature in the raw versus revolution; message through folk melody for women's rights in the rural areas; and the beauteous maiden that the mother earth is. Perennial favourites like *Enniya Mudial Vendum* praying for the national unity to the Almighty*; Olipadaitha Kanninai,* exhorting the youth to guide the country into the future; *Vidudalai Vidudalai* (freedom, freedom), on revoking the yoke of the British colonialism; and Bharati's version of *Vande Mataram* were all soulfully sung and depicted in chorography.

The high point of the evening was the very competent band of dancers that Saroja painstakingly trained, whose energy, verve and evident enthusiasm were equally matched by their clear *adavus* and matching *anga shuddhi*. A word of suggestion to the guru would be to eliminate her many personal appearances — alongside the younger lot – to depict the spirit of Bharati for his beloved motherland. This would do full justice to her undoubted stature, without drawing an unfair comparison.

"I was drawn to Bharati when I was barely 12 or 13 and inspired by his rousing poems," recalls Saroja. "I'd always loved patriotic songs since I saw Gandhi at the age of 9. Bharati's songs were very popular in my times. He had been to Santiniketan to meet Tagore and translated some of the great poet's patriotic poems. I'd choreographed Bharati's *Panchali Shabda*, on her vows of protestations, in 1982-83 and on his thoughts on nature in 1995: on fire (within you and outside); water (rains, ocean and the riverbank, described in his beautiful Tamil ghazal); earth (as mother, seen by a small child); and sky (predicting our reaching moon, a hundred years from his time). I was completely true to the poems on the present occasion, conceptualising music and dance, after reading the verses. We used 36 *Ragas* in all, counting some of the old favourites from earlier times – with solemn *Ragas* for sad lines and light *Ragas* for joyous occasions – including *Mohanam, Kalyan Revathi* and *Bhim Palasi*. We visualised the entire group choreography: with every dancer's entry, exit, presentation and position in the tableau, according to the mood of each poem. We've tried, for instance, to imagine with Bharati, the earth-maiden: with dark pupa in the dusky sky, smiling with the radiance of blooming flowers and revealing a bewitching figure in the hills and valleys: whom the poet wishes to possess!"

Rudra, among the most ancient of the *Vedic* deities, was envisioned by the early seers at least for four millennia and a half, and permitted many forms of devotion. Questioned on *Rudra*'s possible antiquity, Dr. Karan Singh, an authority on tradition and spirituality, puts the notion further back, "The concept was there even during Harappa and

Mohenjo Daro civilisations five millennia ago and gradually took the form of an anthropomorphic god by the *Puranic* times. As my *Ishta Devata* (god for personal worship), I contemplate upon him as: *Om Dhyae Nitya Mahesham.* We find him in three forms: *Shiva Lingam* as the phallic symbol of all creation; and *Dhyana Murti* (meditative figure) seated at Mount Kailash and functioning at the destroying end of the Divine Trinity. But the most endearing one is his third form as dancing *Nataraja,* symbolising the dynamic universe: right from rhythmic movements of galaxies in the macrocosm, to the whirling motions of sub-atomic particles in the microcosm. *Nataraja's* iconic visualisation is superb: with two upper hands holding drum of life and fire of destruction, and two lower hands dispensing benediction and solace…"

Rudram from Yajur Veda, the dance-ballet presented by Saroja Vaidyanathan and students of 'Ganesha Natyalaya', used the compilation of *Mantras* and methods for chant by the priests in performing *Vedic* rituals and *Yajnas* (sacrifices). Explains Saroja, "Out of nearly 4,000 verses of *Yajur Veda,* we have taken the fourth Canto, believed to be its centre-piece and chosen the fifth *Prasana,* namely, the *Rudra-Adhyaya Prasana,* said to be its quintessence." True to the *Vedic* vision, the non-anthropomorphic *Rudra* lords over the elemental forces of nature and dwells in everything: space, air, fire, water and earth!

Splendidly attired in saffron (except the lone male in a jarring creamy vest), the dancers create, dissolve and re-create the five elements. Accompanied by sonorous *Yajur* hymns, composed and sung by Mohan Vaidya from Chennai, *Rudra Puja* was celebrated with primeval mnemonics. *Lam* resonates for earth as *Chandan* (sandalwood); *Ham* for space as *Pushpa* (blossom); *Yam* for wind as *Dhupam* (joss-stick); *Ram* for fire as *Aarati* (icon-worship with burning lamp); and *Vam* for water as *Teertha Prasadam* (holy water from pilgrimage). Prayers to four *Dishas* (directions) have striking body-postures illuminating the stage. Bringing in flora and fauna as symbols, Saroja explains well, "For the *Vedic* era of strong nature-worship, I've used animals, birds and plants as significant symbols, such as, *Tulsi* for Vishnu, *Vilwa Patra* for Shiva, or, bird (*Garuda)* for Vishnu, snake for Shiva, peacock for Kartikeya and swan for Saraswati. Gods in human figures were yet to come and the *Vedas* had no temples either!"

The subsequent narrative on Shiva as Lord of Dance, and the episode of Daksha's daughter immolating herself and Shiva dancing *Tandava,* are well executed, but suffer from confusion in chronology, as they are mythic events of the *Puranic* period coming much, much afterwards! For dovetailing these legends in a programme devoted to *Yajur Veda,* Saroja has a logical defence, "It's true they were later happenings in myths. But we needed them to concentrate on attributes of *Rudra* like fire that comes through beautifully in the Daksha episode or the Ganga story associated with Shiva that illustrates the grandeur of water!" And why bring in forty *Karanas* and four Carnatic rhythms as the finale alongside *Yajur Veda*?

Deep antiquity of *Rudra* gets an unexpected parallel from the Russian danseuse Oxana Chugueva in the group, "We've in my land a millennia-old pagan god *Rod,* whose name is phonetically so close to *Raudra*, — wearing red clothes and fiery in nature, like *Rudra. Rod,* too, sustains life and all living beings." How close can civilisations be, yet so far apart!

Every twelfth day (*Dwadashi*) from the full moon and the new moon time twice a month, tens of thousands of devotees in the south India congregate in the major Shiva temples during the twilight hours: from one hour before the sunset up to the time the moon rises. They offer prayers in their fervent belief that Shiva would dance his *Tandava* in the dusk, — the cosmic dance that would rid the world of ignorance and fetch it wisdom. Aeons ago in mythic times, this was the dance of Shiva that took place in between the horns of Nandi, the divine bull that is his mount! And it was this dance, which was taught by the sage Tandu to Bharata, — with its knowledge forming later the quintessence of the world's most complete performing arts treatise *Natya Shastra* by Bharata. *Pradosham* (the dusk), the dance-drama by Ganesha Natyalaya, presented this fascinating story – of the genesis of all dances and ballets.

Says the director Saroja Vaidyanathan, "In my concept and choreography, my 21 disciples and I begin at the very beginning of things, — when the gods have become effete under the sage Durvasha's curse and the demons threaten to overrun the heaven. The gods direly need *amrita* (nectar) to gain immortality and, under Vishu's counsel, begin churning the primordial ocean: with Mandar Mountain as the churning pole, Vasuki snake as the rope and Vishnu himself in the incarnation of tortoise providing the founding base. This yields profusion of poison and gas from Vasuki's mouth, when everybody turns black. Only Shiva can hold this and he drinks this up: to become *Nilakantha* (blue-throated).

Amidst universal rejoicing, the churning now reveals the goddess Lakshmi, the elephant Airavat, the flying horse Uchchaishrava, the divine blossom Parijat, the boon-giving tree Kalpa Vriksha, the ever-milking cow Kamadhenu and finally, the physician Dhanwantari carrying the bowl of nectar. In the ensuing commotion, Vishnu appears as the enchantress Mohini and, after distributing nectar to the queuing gods, disappears. The frustrated demons give a violent chase and Shiva has to be a saviour again: coming down from his Kailasha abode and dancing *Tandava* on his bull's forehead in the eventide, with Parvati accompanying in *Lasya*. "What a dance it is, — with Vishnu on mridangam, Saraswati on veena, Narada on cymbals, Brahma keeping the rhythm and Lakshmi giving vocal support!"

Saying this, she adds, "That was the fount head of all fine and performing arts, consolidated in *Natya Shastra*. I've tried to use mainly *mime/ Mukhavinaya* (facial expressions) to evoke *rasa*, unlike *Ahariya* in Kathakali and *angika* of hands and legs in Odissi and Kathak. My music is Carnatic, entirely based on Sanskrit verses, using *Ragas* like *Kalyani* and *Revati* for the demons, *Athana* and *Mohanam* for the gods. For *Lasya*, I've used a *Raga* like *Vasanta* and Jatis for *Tandava*. Moods of the *Ragas* are important for me, alongside instruments like veena, violin, morseng and flute. It's mainly group choreography, — with main characters like Shiva, Parvati, Nandi and Vishnu strung together on a narrative by Narada. I've drawn the relevance from the fact that the origin of our dances is so little known and it's worth an effort to take dance beyond glamour and entertainment, — to their roots."

Justin McCarthy's Group

AND THE TWAIN SHALL MEET: *Justin McCarthy*

The joint performance of Dhrupad by Nirmalya Dey and Bharatanatyam by Justin McCarthy (with Lokesh Bharadwaj) at the Alliance Françoise was a unique get-together between the North and the South. The 13th century had provided the watershed years in the music of this sub-continent when Carnatic music assumed colours different from its Hindustani counterpart. While the devotional *Keertanam* and composed *Kritis* by Purandara Dasa, Kshetrangya and the 'musical trinity' of Thyagaraja, Shyama Sastry and Muthuswamy Dexter began dominating the South over the following centuries, music across the Vindhyas went for Dhrupad by the 15th century, inspired by Mansingh Tomar (and his wife Mriganayani) of Gwalior and, by the next century came the ascetic-composer Swami Haridas giving Dhrupad its glory: with a galaxy of disciples like Mian Tansen, Baiju Bawara and Gopal Naik: whose names and contributions are still remembered. The texts of Dhrupad – mostly written in Braj language — include philosophy, mythology, nature and various aspects of music and life, and bears testimony to the treasure-trove of literary values that was handed down from the medieval India, before the free-wheeling Khayal appeared on the scene in later years.

It was, therefore, fascinating to come to the meeting point of two distinctive cultures: the Dagar Vani gharana of Dhrupad and the well-demarcated Kalakshetra style of Bharatanatyam. Nirmalya presented a late-afternoon *Raga Bhim Palasi,* followed by a Dhamar in *Raga Des: Jhulana-me Racho Raas:* to recall the festival of colour, — in the impeccable *Beenkar Ang* of his guru Ustad Zia Fariduddin Dagar with *Alaap, Jod* and *Jhala,* as sung with vocal syllables. Articulation of the *Bandish* (lyric) and its *Upaj* (improvisation) was marked with different intensities in *Shrutis* (microtones) to establish the *Ragas*.

Then joined Justin in a *Jai Jayanti* composition: *Main Hun Chita Chahata Piya-se Milawe-ko*: and yet another in *Raga Sohini*: *Prathama Adi Shiva Shakti.* The dance sequences were evidently inspired by music, but not synchronised with it: allowing the luxuriant and relaxed *Alaap* to take its course. While the first composition brought out free association with *Sahitya* (literature) – etching images of Yamuna, the flute-playing cowherd-god and the eager wait for the tryst by the milkmaids – the second item showcased a very vigorous *Shiva Tandava*: with all the attributes of the fearsome god in their effulgent glory.

Nirmalya is mindful of his heritage, "The aesthetics and significance of Dhrupad – vocal or instrumental – are laid down in the venerable treatises like *Sangeet Ratnakara, Sangeet Parijata* and *Sangeet Darshana* of the Middle Ages. Ours is the classical genre – earlier denied to women as *Mardana Gayaki* – not to entertain, but for self-realisation." Justin is equally emphatic on the spirit of collaboration, "The approach is kept open-ended: to maintain integrity and dignity of both music and dance. Whenever the two forms come together, it's because there is a common foundation. Yet, improvisations play a big role: inspired by the clarity of *Shruti* and the simplicity of the literary allusions, — our convergences and divergences on the platform have a fair amount of chance-element!"

FROM MULTI-MEDIA TO MAHADEVA: *Revanta Sarabhai*

Do the genes speak? When the legendary choreographer-scholar Mrinalini Sarabhai and her globally-famous daughter Mallika Sarabhai held their annual *Darpana Festival* a few years back, they were accompanied by the teenager Revanta, Mallika's son, who had then begun multi-media studies in Philadelphia. The budding youth enacted the little Krishna embracing amorously the charming Radha: none other than Mrinalini. The doting grandmother had commented

Revanta Sarabhai

then lightly, "It made perfect sense, because all grannies anecdotally proposition their progeny!"

The genes spoke again when the three generations came back in Delhi: with the octogenarian Mrinalini as affectionate spectator, Mallika a spirited compere, and Revanta – all of 23 and fresh from the States with a 4-year degree from University of the Arts, and several design and multimedia projects under his belt – putting up a brilliant dance-recital centred on Shiva. It was an emphatic epiphany of the genes, as Mallika confides, "I always dissuaded Revanta from dance, despite the ambience around him. But, when he was 5 and I'd just returned from a long Western tour with the epic-play *Mahabharata*, he walked up to me and declared that he was going to dance! Notwithstanding all his fascinations for convergence technology, he has not looked back since." But the younger sibling, Anahita, has surely not taken to dance? Smiles Mallika, "That was true earlier when I put her up in the University of Griffith in Australia. But she'd stayed barely a week, didn't attend any class and, by the time I was to fly in to settle her down, she came back to Ahmedabad. That's seven days now and she's declared she'd like to dance in 'Darpana' hereafter." So the genes have asserted finally!

Groomed in Bharatanatyam by Mrinalini and guru Maheshwari Nagarajan, Revanta opened with a captivating *Kauthuvam* – comprising both *Nritta* and *Abhinaya* – dedicated to Ganesha, Kartikeya and Nataraja in *Raga Malka*. Revanta's tall and lissome body was an apt tool for dance, — resonating with rhythmic syllables intertwined with the lyrics eulogising the gods and their attributes. In many senses, his solo debut resembled the advent of Uday Shankar in the 30's: with lush long hair, a superbly-toned body and a command over extraordinarily fluid gestures. "I've been compared to Ram Gopal before," laughs Revanta. "My height falls short of six-foot by half-an-inch and I always teased Mom why she didn't eat more Protein when she was expecting, so that I could be a six-footer!"

Varnam, the mainstay of Bharatanatyam repertoire, was in *Raga Natakurunji,* extolling glorious virtues of Shiva: as the supreme, the saviour, the compassionate one, the knowledge-giver and the joyous dancer. The diligent learning of the pristine *Pandannalur* style showed off in the clear body-lines and uncluttered movements. Confirms Revanta, "Since the inception of 'Darpana' in 1949, Mrinalini had insisted on retaining purity of *Pandannalur* due to its refined balance of *Tandava, Lasya* and *Shringara,* very different from the cuddly *Vazhuvoor* style!" Adds he reflectively, "Amma taught me calm and gracefulness. Although my *Varnam* —and other pieces — go back to a couple of centuries in composition, I fall back on my teaching to mould them in my way. It's important for me to decide how I look; respond and not copy form the ancestry."

The *Abhinaya* pieces were the famous *Padam: Nadanam Adinar:* in *Raga Vasanta* and the *Bhajan* on Shamkara Srigiri in *Raga Hamnndi.* As ode to Mahadeva, the former was etched in crystalline lines of *Tandava* while the latter accented *Lasya,* with the kinaesthetics filling up the chamber theatre in their outreach. Answering how Revanta, as a modern youth, adjusts to the vision of divinity in the dancer expected by viewers for such items, concedes he, "I'm not particularly religious nor do I go to temples to say my prayers. Yet, I find the themes here reveal a spiritual core that I can treat as metaphors. I'm proud of being born a Hindu, hut want to rise above the vulgar exhibitionism that is often imputed to it today!" Warming up to his perception of dance vis-à-vis his multimedia proficiency, elaborates Revanta, "I did an installation-art, *Please Touch,* in a Philadelphia gallery, where I attempted to break barriers between museums and their visitors, — by making three dancers perform in the centre-space and improvising to buttons or slides the audience would activate. Thus, the stimulus of blue, green or red light would make performers keep changing their response. I got high accolade and realised the tremendous potential of multimedia to create novel performative experiences!" On design, "I'm working to bring graphic design into mainstream choreography: to improve aesthetics through composition (emptiness or filling the stage), balance (slow or fast) and energy-level." Revanta views future with prescience, "I've already worked with dance-theatre in my solo, *Eklavya,* exploring how education is denied to the underprivileged, and *Transposed Heads,* based on Karnad's *Hayavadana,* on crisis of identity. I recently performed, for the NSD festival, in the dance-theatre adaptation of the Greek-play, *Phaedra,* under Astrid Bas from France and find such extensions hugely exciting!"

ELOQUENCE OF STATUESQUE STANCE:
Priya Venkataraman

Priya Venkataraman

Ancient Tamil literature provides probably the richest literary tradition in India, no less than the Sanskrit legacy, in quality and variety. Great poetry from the *Sangam* period (100 BC – 500 AD) comprised several anthologies of exquisitely-written emotional poems, often surprisingly secular and revealing depths of poetic feelings. The post-*Sangam* literature included *Thirukkural,* a splendid work of 1,330 verses, by the weaver-writer Thiruvaluvar, on ethics and *Dharma,* to be followed by both family-men and saints. There were five great epics, known together as 'Tamil Quintet', including *Silappadikaram,* that appeared by the end of the 2nd century AD.. By the 7th century, there was the genre of Vaishnavite *Bhakti* poetry by Alvars, comprising thousands of verses (*Prabandham*), — followed by the other tradition of *Thevaram*, the song-cycles contributed by the Shaivaite poets around the 9th-10th century. The reformist Shaivaite movement of the 12th century led to emergence of another kind of lyrical-philosophical poetry….

Old Poetry, New Frame was a small cross-section of this astonishingly rich poetic heritage, presented through Bharatanatyam *Margam* (set-repertoire) by young and petite Priya Venkataraman. Her performance had three inherent advantages, namely, a total dedication to the pristine purity of her form; a carefully honed solo choreography that suited her movements; and a heightened sensibility to the aesthetic beauty of the verses born out of her sustained exposure to the West for years. But the best advantage was the elegance of her tall, lissome stature that added special piquancy to the poetic nuances in all five items that she chose to present, especially in *Varnam,* the central piece. Says Priya, "It's the work of an old saint-poet which I've choreographed for myself, by keeping in mind the moods of my own and the movements that suited my body-type, my steps and my flexibility. I've realised that the choreography by gurus may or may not suit every disciple of theirs."

The advantages were brought home right from the beginning. The invocation in Sanskrit, composed by Shahji Maharaj, the 16th century Marathi ruler of Tanjavoor, was in *Raga Natai: Shule Yuta Shovita Vani, Shumbha-Nishumbha Mardini*…. Priya came into her own in Tamil *Varnam* in *Raga Charukesi* on an impassioned plea to the divine lover: *You act as if you're unaware of how I feel*… and ambled the stage with infinite grace, never allowing the spirit to sag. Endorses she, "I didn't want to make the *Varnam* heavy and adhered to the strict dictum that I don't repeat myself!" A Jayadeva *Ashtapadi* followed in *Raga Bageshri: Sa Virahe Tabalina Madhava*…, then a *Padam* by saint Surayananda in *Raga Sindhu Bharavi: Gangadhishwaram Shankaram*…and a final *Tillana* by Ponnaiya Pillai in *Raga Kedaram.*

Yet the million-dollar question remained to be asked: Why does she not use her prowess in technique and grammar to interpret modern poetry? After all, seminal contribution to Tamil literature is going on through new writings and that feature in magazines like *Kalki, Kumudam, Ananda Vikatan* and *Swadesha Mitran.* Why does one not visualise those gems, — beyond the ken of *Bhakti-Shringara* and *Prem-Shringara*? Priya agrees whole-heartedly, "Now that I'm without guru, I want to break away from *Margam* and take on new poems from possibly the new year." Good luck to her!

LEGACY OF BALA SARASWATI: *Uma Vasudevan*

Uma Vasudevan

Do genes speak? For a Bharatanatyam danseuse like Uma Vasudevan, who is the seventh generation in her family to continue the tradition of performing arts, is there a built-in genetic reserve of energy and enthusiasm, interest and involvement with the muses, right from the birth? Before giving her sparkling shows at different venues, Uma recalls, "My great-great grandmother was Veenai Dhanammal, the most celebrated veena-player of her era. My grandmother T Mukhta and her sister T Brinda formed a formidable singing-duo who stormed Tamil Nadu musical scene, besides composing numerous *Padams* (songs) and *Javalis* (erotic poetry). My great-aunt was the legendary T Bala Saraswati whose powerful influence has endured as my heritage." Endorses the well-known Kuchipudi dancer Swapna Sundari about Mukhta, "I was her student from 1985 to 1992 when I was doing Bharatanatyam. She was benign but not meek, and could be a hard taskmaster by insisting on checking the singing quality of a fresh disciple before agreeing to teach *Padams*. Uma and I learnt to dance together with some of her most unforgettable songs."

The lineage was evident, right from the word go. In the opening *Dashavatara Stotra* by Annamcharya, the 14th century poet, Uma's was a sparkling performance to depict ten incarnations of Vishnu, which surprisingly included both Krishna and Balarama, but excluded the Buddha. This was in sharp contrast to the more celebrated 'Ode to *Dashavatara'* by Jayadeva which regards Krishna as manifest God and, therefore, not an incarnation. Again Swapna offers a logical explanation, "Annamacharya came some 300 years after Jayadeva, when concepts of the incarnations had radically changed. Buddhism was a spent force in the south by then and our poet could ignore him!"

Uma was obviously at ease with both Tanjavoor and Vazhuvoor styles of her dance, as was seen in her elaborate *Varnam,* in *Raga Malika,* to a Subramania Bharati composition of modern period, which depicts the confident and outspoken heroine who lashes out at the fooling around by her hero and yet retains her self-respect, after having spoken her heart out. The form used was *Ninda-Stuti* (praise through deprecation). The *Abhinaya* was clearly a gift from her redoubtable guru Kalanidhi Narayan, but the Bala stamp of expressions and gestures was also unmistakably there. Admits a modest Uma, "I'm doing all I can to keep Bala's good name in my expressional work, but I'm also hugely helped by my immediate family." This was amply borne out by her musical support: Mridangam by husband Vasudevan, *Nattubhangam* (conducting) and flute by brothers-in-law Elangovan and Raghuraman, and vocals by sister-in-law Sudha: a total family affair!

The two *Padams* – in Tamil and Telugu – that followed were in *Ragas Saveri* and a pensive *Sahana.* The first describes an enraged heroine who detects a lover two-timing her, with tale-tell marks of the nightly dalliance and dried coliseum, and wishes he should just go away. The sentiment was much alike the famous Jayadeva *Ashtapadi: Yahi Madhava Yahi Keshava...,* although on a more sarcastic note and not specifically driving him into the waiting arms of the 'other woman'! The second song questioned the follies of a married woman following her heart's dictates and defying the honour of those around, — an eternal problem of *amour propre*! The concluding *Javali,* in *Raga Paraz,* was appropriately fast-paced.

The surprising part was the pristine pure adherence to Bala-like tradition that Uma reflected, despite her decade-and-a-half life in Canada. "I'm 41 and have a school with French students, too. But I adhere to my own legacy of classical *Margam* (repertoire) without the need for experiments, at least not yet. The nearest innovation we've done is a *Jati-Laya-Sarasa* where Vasudevan articulates mnemonics and plays mridangam while I dance, — somewhat like Kathak. We'd love to do it in India!"

FRAGRANCE FROM FRANCE: *Rebecca*

If the Indian field of sports has been a great leveller for all religions, belying the Pakistan skipper's claim to the contrary for the Islamic world, post- T20 World Cup, — there is another arena which has long learnt to make religious affiliation irrelevant: Indian performing arts. While reverence for goddesses Kali and Saraswati has been legendarily there for Ustad Bismilla Khan and Baba Allauddin Khan of yore, one never comes back from Puri's gargantuan *Ratha Yatra* without listening over the public address system the songs of *Ninda-Stuti* (deprecatory praise) by Salah Beg, the Muslim disciple of Jagannath, or, return from Vrindavan's *Raas Lila* and Krishna-*Bhakti* gatherings without hearing the Brij music by Ras Khan, the Arab devotee of Krishna who was debarred once from entering the Lord's temple. The Dagar brothers, Ustad Naseeruddin and Ustad Faiyazuddin, always regaled listeners at home with soulful rendering of Dhamar music on Radha-Krishna theme and the latest chanting from *Atharva Veda* by Ustad Salimulla Khan at Drishtikon Kathak festival was just another case in point.

Leela Samson, the celebrated Bharatanatyam danseuse now heading 'Kalakshetra' in Chennai, comes from the Jewish family of Admiral Samson, the ex-Naval chief and now wafts in Rebecca from France like a whiff of fresh air, in that illustrious lineage. Dancing for the first time in India, says Rebecca, all of 25, "I do come from a Jewish family which observes all major rituals and festivals of our religion Yet my mother, Annie, has been learning Kathakali from 'Kalamandalam' since 1986 and coming to India every year with me tucked in as a child! Now for a decade, she is Sadanan Balakrishnan's disciple and commutes among Paris, Chennai and Delhi to keep up with him. My father, Hilbert, teaches neurology and is a professional psychoanalyst, but he practises yoga in Rishikesh for weeks together every now and then. I've been learning Bharatanatyam since I was 8 from Malavika, the first French dancer of my genre."

Rebecca, disciple of Jamuna Krishnan since 2003, proved her proficiency with a traditional repertoire. After a *Pushpanjali* in *raga Natai,* she executed an elaborate *Varnam: Vana Jaksha,* composed by TR Muthu Tandava, in *Raga Behag,* on the lotus-eyed goddess. Next was a *Padam* in *Raga Khamaj,* on a *nayika* in love with Shiva, followed by a *Nirguna Bhajan* by Kabir in *Raga Rageshwari*: *Hamso rahiyo na jaye, murli ki dhun suni ke....* There is an unusual Surdas *Bhajan: Hari, yun murli tumhe sunau...,* where Radha proposes role-reversal with Krishna, asking for his cross-dressing in her clothes This was an eye-catcher in *raga-malika.* The finale was a fast *Tillana* in *Raga Bageshri.* Perhaps Rebecca deserves a choreography more suiting her Western physique, until she evolves her own.

Adds Rebecca, "Although I'm a music graduate in Western violin from Germany, I love Indian mythology." About her disparate background, she avers, "I believe in one world and different ways to approach one God. Europe views God and art in a fundamentally different manner. There I'm still Rebecca on the platform. On Indian stage, I'm a tiny Rebecca, only a medium for a superior energy! To me, life today is unimaginable without India and without dance which comes to me naturally as a mother's daughter!"

WHITHER BHARATANATYAM? *Maria Kiron, Divya Saluja*

They are both bright young things. Maria Kiran is 25, has already done 10 years in Bharatanatyam under Guru Jamuna Krishnan, and a few earlier years' training in Paris. Having completed her schooling from abroad, she has skipped the university education and given herself entirely to the classical form. Divya Saluja is all of 23, has been with Bharatanatyam guru Geeta Chandran for 15 years, and, having done graduation in Economics Honours, is studying for MBA. Maria, settled in France, commutes very frequently to India to keep up her chosen grooming, while Divya, based in Delhi, combines

Maria Kiron

studies with training, and has kept her professional options open still. Both are excellently turned-out dancers, — revealing a palpable dedication and enthusiasm that is infectious. Now, the hard question is: where do their gurus see them 5 years or 10 years hence?

Says a demure Maria in French-flavoured English, "I'm keen on *Margam* that provides me standard item-sequence. Each dancer picks up *Margam* from the teacher in her own way and constantly adds to the repertoire. I don't think a traditional *Margam* is ever boring to the viewer, provided, the dancer can contribute that extra sparkle." But is being located in France a help or a hindrance? "You won't know how much Europeans love tradition, missing it in their contemporary arts! For the last three years, I'm performing in Theatre de Bille, the largest Parisian stage and its erudite director, Gerard Violette, who is very conscientious and has been to India, has asked me to perform on four evenings as soon as I'm back. This, I consider, is real appreciation!"

As things went, Maria's *Margam* was scintillating. A *Pushpanjali* was followed by an elaborate V*arnam* on *Shringarta Rasa* in *Raga Natya Kuranji.* This was followed by an uncommon Tamil *Padam* in *raga Begati.* Then came a vibrant Vidyapati lyric: *Aaj Pekhalu Nanda Kishora:* set by her guru in the lilting *Raga Shivaranjini.* The finale was a Lalgudi Jayaraman *Tillana* in *Raga Bageshri.* Asked the question on her future, avers guru Jamuna, "She has been a fine disciple, intent on picking up the base, grammar, technique and nuances of Bharatanatyam. I think she is blooming well." On doing her own choreography yet, which she would need for her sustenance, Jamuna comments cautiously, "I'm giving her foundation and understanding and the ability to look back to the basics. She's very passionate about her dance and is receiving the right encouragement from the French arts authorities. Her home 'Mandava' is a haven for all Indian artists visiting France, and support from her adoptive parents Roger and Melina is very deep. I do see a great future for her!"

The tall and lissome Divya is more forthright in her opinion, "Bharatanatyam is something that connects to spirituality. My guru has defined for me almost a way of life. My academic choice may give me a different world, but my dance is also a choice as it gives me amalgamation to truth!" On whether Bharatanatyam would take her far, she pauses, "Traditional dance is always alluring for me and I'm sure people are increasingly realising the value of classical arts. Even *Margam* can be done in a myriad ways." And on the potential for experimentation, "I'll stick to classical substance and perhaps not venture into new content, — unless it echoes an awakening in my audience who understands Bharatanatyam and yet seeks a contemporary theme!" Divya's presentation of *Margam* was exemplar. After a prayer to Ganesha in *Raga Des,* she performed a *Mallari,* inspired by a deity's entourage of musical instruments during a ceremonial procession, followed by a slowly-opening *Alarippu* and a Papanasam Shivan composition in the beautiful *Raga Hamsadhwani.* Then came the *Varnam* dominated by *Shringara Rasa,* in *raga Natya Kuranji.* After a Gopala Krishna Bharati *Padam* in *Raga Todi* came the concluding *Tillana* by Dandayudhapani Pillai in *Raga Hindolam* with excellent, exuberant movements.

On where does Divya go from here, responds guru Geeta not too optimistically, "She cherishes her dance, but given the non-transparency of the system and the rigid structure, opportunities do seem very few. Yes, they do get a chance to give a hand in choreography and contribute to items in new productions in our 'Natya Vriksha'. They also get a wide range of vocabulary even within traditional *Margam.* But solo opportunities are rare, and they're pushed into group choreography, which does not do justice to their individual talents. One doesn't know what the yeas will show!"

BRINGING ARTS TO A CHILD: *Mamata Niyogi-Nakra*

The laudable aim of the seminar, organised under Kala Bharati of Canada, was to share with a wide group of viewers the ideas and findings of four qualified and experienced artists in the fields of dance, music, puppetry and painting, who have been involved in making their respective arts 'child-friendly'. As was pointedly observed, Plato exhorted in Greece millennia ago that the child should be taught only music, physics and philosophy. In India, Bhaskaracharya initiated Lilavati into mathematics through music and dance in the 6th century. Over the years, academic subjects became immune from the embalming touch of the arts. Even classical dance and music grew to make no concessions for the child, because, in the traditional context, these were areas of expertise where amateurs had no place. It was ruefully commented that India's great gurus perhaps never thought of a child-friendly repertoire in classical dances, supported by child-friendly music! Every time one watched a youngster wrestle with complicated rhythmic sequences in a performance and found the child struggle with adult emotions of the stereotyped *Nayika,* one experienced only two things: either, a body-mind separation in the child totally isolated from what the dance and music were meant to show; or, a precocious imitation of adult mannerisms. Why have more teachers not thought in terms of fashioning a special repertoire: more in empathy with the child's perception of the world?

As a backgrounder, it was elaborated how dance, by itself, helped a child's verbal, kinesthetic, spatial and inter-personal intelligence: besides IQ and EQ. Mamata Niyogi-Nakra, founder-chief of Kala Bharati, presented audio-visually *Shishu Sadhana,* the complete child-friendly Bharatanatyam repertoire that she had fashioned in Montreal in the last few years. She explained the process covering the *Margam: Aradhana, Alarippu, Jatiswaram, Shabdam,* an elaborate *Varnam,* three *Padams* and a scintillating *Tillana.* The difficult *Varnam,* for instance, was about the dancer waking up a friendly giant with many tricks: tickling, sprinkling water and setting the buzzing bee buzz around around its nose…

The *Shabdam* was based on a kid's letter to Shiva posing innocent questions: how did the Lord live in the cold Kailasha, warm himself with a mere tiger-skin, and swallow water overcoming the poison deposited in his throat? In another *Padam,* the child coddled her little doll, despaired in having lost it for a while and was ultimately overjoyed in finding it back! The *Tillana* thrived upon a series of animal movements, familiar to the children, namely, the strutting peacock, majestic elephant, prowling crocodile, swimming fish and hissing snake. The musician OS Arun explained that *Ragas* like *Shankarabharanam, Todi, Bhairavi* and *Saveri* – with elaborate *Gamakas* – were avoided in *Shishu Sadhana*, favouring *Hamsadhwani:* with catchy *Swaras.* .

While Kala Bharati's was indeed the most path-breaking endeavour donc halfway across the globe in this genre, it appeared that some piecemeal work has also been done in this country. Kalakshetra took early steps to make tradition suitable to the children. Guru Dandayudhapani Pillai saw the absurdity of a child executing a *Varnam* with its full-blown *Shringara* and composed a simple *Varnam:* showing a mother-child relationship. Birju Maharaj evolved *Tihais* and *Tukras* woven around 'rasagullas' or round rhythms from daily-life activity like attending telephone-rings. Leela Samson, director of Kalakshetra, had taught youngsters by linking the gesture-vocabulary with ideas familiar to the child or having simple poems danced by them. Pushkala Gopal, the Bharatanatyam danseuse, did the same with students of Sardar Patel Vidyalaya. Suchitra Mitra taught in Chandigarh the 3-year olds frog jumping: in order to learn rhythmic steps.

Kanaka Sudhakar brought out therapeutic benefits of dance for a child. Having worked for remedying neurological disorders and achieving better mind-body coordination, she averred that dance could help 'slow learners' to perform rapid alternative movements and left-right hand-associations in the age-bracket of 4-5 and 'mirror' movements for children aged 5-17. All this while, the brain functions improved, — with better visual recognition, spatial perception and mathematical felicity, alongside learning of languages. With observations based on experimental children as well as control-group children of equal size, the insights offered were most valuable.

The Puppeteer Varun Narain demonstrated endearingly – with live example of Selma, the Bunraku puppet — how to make puppets child-friendly and instill belief in magic. The finale was Shantnu Chakraborty delightful selection of children's paintings: drawn around the *Shishu Sadhana* themes. As was tellingly brought out, a child was basically art-friendly, as a little one danced spontaneously without following the tenets of *Shringara,* or, doodled on any available medium without a clue to a painter's sense of proportions! Possibly all one needed was, one, a *triggering point*: to catch a child's attention and give him a nudge of surprise; two, a *critical mass*: where the child's interaction and involvement with the art form would become comprehensive, as, say, in a puppet-play; and, three, a *finesse:* where there would be no compromise on the artistic quality, as achieved, for instance, in *Shishu Sadhana* repertoire. The involvement and enjoyment of the child with the arts would then be complete and unreserved!

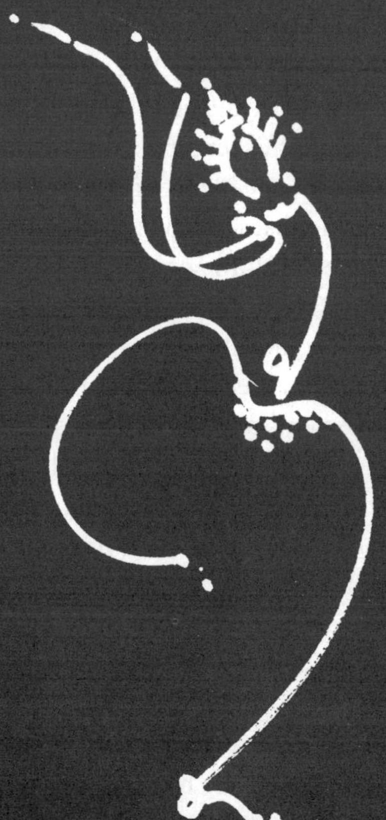

Odissi

Madhavi Mudgal

Overview

by Madhavi Mudgal

The lyrical, sensuous classical dance style, known as Odissi today, belongs to the eastern part of the country, and is referred to in the *Natya Shastra* as Odra-Magadhi. It is characterised by undulating torso movements and gait which transform seamlessly into varying patterns that are typical of the region's culture.

Odissi traces its roots at least to the 2nd century BC, through archaeological and textual evidence. Although it existed in some form or the other through the centuries, it is difficult to say exactly what form it took Post independence in 1947. At the time of its reconstruction, this style that is known as Odissi today, sought its roots in the living dance tradition of the Gotipuas (boy-dancers) as well as the almost extinct Mahari (temple devadasis) tradition. Insightful gurus and scholars also found the Orissa's sculptural legacy (particularly within the temples) to be a major resource for devising the movements and positions to be used in dance. In Orissa, people with a talent for dance normally found an outlet in popular Oriya theatre before Odissi emerged as an independent form. Most of the girls pursuing dance at that time learnt other styles like Bharatanatyam, Kathak, or even Uday Shankar style.

After the 1950's, Odissi was established as a new style in the classical field. Priyambada Mohanty and Indrani Rahman were able to arouse initial curiosity in the 1960's while Sanjukta Panigrahi, Kumkum Das, Sonal Mansingh and some others brought about a serious interest in the 1970's and 1980's when it became immensely popular. Ground-breaking work was done by the senior Gurus in terms of structuring the form and creating new pieces. A lot of established dancers of other styles were attracted by Odissi and chose to add an item or two to their repertoire. Dedicated exponents of Odissi presented full-length performances to much acclaim from connoisseurs. It was not so much in Orissa, but in Delhi that Odissi performances were held initially. Gurus like Mayadhar Raut and Hare Krishna Behera settled and taught in Delhi, while Guru Kelucharan Mohapatra held regular workshops. Subsequently, Guru Ramani Ranjan Jena went to Chennai, Shankar Behera to Mumbai and Murlidhar Majhi to Kolkata, to start Odissi classes. In Orissa institutes like Kala Vikas Kendra, National Music Association and Utkal Sangeet Mahavidyalaya did pioneering work, as a result of which we see today a large number of gurus and dancers within this form.

It was in 1985 that 'Angahar', a landmark festival of Odissi, was organised by the Gandhara Mahavidyalaya, New Delhi. It brought together all the major gurus, scholars and exponents of the dance form, including representations from the Gotipuas and Mahari traditions for the first time. This enabled an assessment of the development of this form since its revival. Initially it was the solo format that brought Odissi to the fore. The repertoire of Odissi usually lasted for about two hours. A *Mangalacharan* and a couple of *Pall avis*, the *Dashavatara* and the detailed presentation of the *Ashtapadis* formed the core of the presentation. Oriya songs were rarely presented, though many dance-dramas were choreographed in Orissa that had Oriya literary content.

The music was a blend of the Hindustani and the Karnataka, but with a typical Oriya flavour: Most Oriya musicians learnt either the Hindustani or the Karnatak styles. Unfortunately, traditional forms of Odissi music like *Champu*, *Chhanda* and *Janana* were rarely presented at music concerts, though this trend has changed recently. There was a lacuna in terms of musical forms available for dance, especially form *Nritta* (abstract) items. Even the *Talas* and basic *Bols* (syllables) had to be culled from unstructured material. Except for lilting Oriya songs which were not necessarily *Raga*-based, composers had to resort to the Hindustani or Karnatak mode, where the structure of a *Raga* was required as a base.

Today, three main styles have emerged within Odissi, representing the three major gurus that were involved in the restructuring of the form: Gurus Pankaj Charan Das, Deba Prasad Das and Kelucharan Mohapatra. Guru Pankaj Charan Das' style carries forward the Mahari tradition; Guru Deba Prasad Das' has a robust and somewhat rustic feel, while Guru Kelucharan Mohapatra, the most prolific and influential of them all, has a very intricate and filigreed treatment both in the abstract and expressional aspects.

In the last few years, the principality of the solo format seems to be receding, to be replaced sadly by a plethora of increasingly tableau-like group work. Often, full-length solo performances do not have foray even in Orissa; partly due to organiser's demands for so-called 'new' work. This is somewhat disquieting and even alarming to the connoisseur, because our tradition allows for any amount of creativity within its framework. However, this does not detract from some very interesting group choreographies that have emerged from serious dancers and gurus. Many choreographers incorporate Gotipua dancers and Chhau elements to enrich presentations, though one feels that this should be done with discrimination and aesthetics in mind. Fusion attempts with Western contemporary have rarely proved successful. Attempts at incorporating Oriya literature in dance is a welcome and satisfying trend. It is only a few who seek the roots of the form to forge newer directions.

The need of the hour is the creation of a discerning and demanding audience including the media, so that a serious work, particularly in the solo format is sustained, and the art evolves into another dimension. It would be a pity if the aspiration for excellence is lost in the jungle of ignorance.

AURA OF ARCHETYPAL WOMEN: *Sonal Mansigh*

Against multiple *yonis* (vaginas) etched on the large Indian map and projected on the cyclorama, *Tejaswini,* presented by Sonal Mansingh, the celebrated dancer and culture-activist, was an inspired choreography, — portraying ten ladies of rare stature, both from mythic and modern times. Says Sonal, "There're many women: known and unknown, famous and unsung, who appeared in the corridors of Indian history and legends, and have since become symbols for a noble, courageous and truthful identity. They're the true inheritors of female power and social transformation." Adds she, "I choreographed them in the early 1990's and produced them piecemeal from time to time, but we still need to remember these archetypal persons holistically as metaphors available for our emulation."

Ahalya sets off, in *Raga Des,* the sky imagery, for the sage Gautama's neglected wife, who exercises her right to sex and accepts Indra's affections, goes into a deep trance under Goutama's curse and wakes up to life under Rama's benign touch. *Tara* is depicted, invoking

Sonal Mansigh

the wind imagery in *Raga Kirwani,* as the spirited consort of the monkey-king Bali who defies Rama whose single arrow then pierces seven palm trees and kills her husband. *Kunti* as 'Pritha' symbolises earth in *Raga Yaman* and uses her right to conceive by the gods at her will: both as a virgin and as a married woman, after wedlock to an impotent Pandu, — to have, as sons, the mighty Pandavas. *Mandodari,* the chief consort of Ravana, is created in *Raga Darbari* using the water image, who bemoans the demon's infatuation with the human Sita. *Draupadi* is the fiery princess from the fires and is seen, in *Raga Hamsadhwani,* to condemn Kauravas to perdition in wrathful revenge for her ignominy. Sonal's choreography is in mellow Odissi wedded to virile Chhau.

After a *Kedar* interlude, the modern period dawns with Madam Bhikaji Kama, who unfurls India's tri-colour flag for the first time in a mega-gathering in 1907, with the song: *Ek Des Ek Bhasha, Ek Jati Ek Asha,* in *Raga Hamsadhwani* and *Bande mataram* in *Des.* Follows Kasturba Gandhi, without whom Mahatma Gandhi might not have succeeded in thoughts and deeds, and yet became a *Brahmachari* later. "The country has chosen to forget Kasturba, 'the musk-deer', beyond naming a short stretch of road after her," laments Sonal. *Sarojini Naidu,* named *Rudra Kokila* (Valiant Cuckoo) by Bapu-*ji,* comes next in *Raga Arbi. Indira Gandhi* is remembered in *Raga Rageshwari*. Declares the dancer, "in the pan-Indian panoply, she showed rare valour and love for the soil of her motherland." The finale is a delightful *Every Woman* in an Ashok Chakradhar poem: *Watan Ki Nari Hoon...,* set to *Raga Prathama Manjari.* Endorses Sonal, "Every woman, rich or poor, urban or rural, deserves her place in the sun and a celebration that she exists!"

"*Tejaswini* carries forward the resolution, of dedicating my art to the nation, that began two decades ago," recalls she. "I belong to a family of Gandhian freedom-fighters, beginning from my grandfather Mangaldas Pakvasa who practised law with Jinnah and Bhulabahi Desai, and gave up everything to strive for freedom. He and my parents moulded my ideals and I inherit their legacy: reflected in my dance- creations and presented every Republic Day on issues lying at our society's core."

DANCE'S OTHER DIMENSIONS: *Ileana Citaristi*

In the firmament of Odissi, Kelucharan Mahapatra – with his scintillating choreography – has been a lodestar for long. After his demise, his disciples have been valiantly carrying on the great legacy and often have added new extensions to the existing oeuvre of the guru. Madhavi Mudgal in Delhi, Jhelum Paranjape in Mumbai, Sharmila Biswas in Kolkata, and Ratikanta Mohapatra, Kumkum Mohanti and Ileana Citaristi in Bhuvaneswar are some of the names that come to one's mind who have held forth the bastion.

Out of them, Ileana's recent performance is a pointer to the directions the style is taking. After a *Mangala Charanam*, as ode to the Sun, three compositions reveal the new strands. First, there is a new and elaborate *Pallavi* in *Raga Bakula Bharanam.* Second, *Ganga Yamuna* as *Abhinaya* draws from Kalidasa's *Raghu Vamsam* and describes Rama and Sita's aerial view of the two rivers flowing towards confluence in striking similes: as two strings of white and black pearls; two pairs of white and black lilies; two flocks of white and black swans flying to Mansarovar lake; and two streaks of white ash and black coiling snake on Shiva's body. Finally, another *Abhinaya* piece *Chitrangada* from the epic *Mahabharata,* depicts the Manipuri princess's fight with Arjuna and, at the touch of the Pandava hero, her newly awakened femininity. "While I retain

Ileana Citaristi

the purity of Kelubabu's approach in presenting his oeuvre, I do use abundant space, and graft metaphors, suggestions and abstractions into my choreography," declares Ileana.

But she is distinctly unhappy at the lack of opportunity in India to work as an artist-in-residence, for a full season, in other professional companies where one can try out novel ideas and experiments, — as is routinely done in the West. Ileana muses, "Working with the film medium, on specific invitation, has been rewarding in that sense over the last ten years. I did choreography for Aparna Sen's *Yuganta;* M F Hussain's *Meenakshi: A Tale of Three Cities;* and Goutam Ghose's *Abar Aranye.* Only in films have I been able to push my dancers beyond their style and unshackle them from their genre. Since I've grounding in theatre under Grotowsky of Poland, I've used elements of theatre movement in my dance repertoire, such as, Greek mythology and Zen-inspired Haiku poems."

She warms up to describe how, after a gap of 25 years, she came in intimate touch with International School of Theatre Anthropology n Europe. "ISTA is running for a couple of decades by the celebrated theatre director Eujenio Barba whose world-famous Odin group has been active in Denmark for nearly half a century," adds Ileana. "Their need of expounding Indian tradition, earlier met by Sanjukta Panigrahi, has now come my way in both 2004 and 2005: involving the teaching of our dance-theatre to 40-45 international participants. Barba last came to attend Padatik's festival on 'Dance, Theatre and Martial Arts' in Kolkata under the thespian Shyamanand Jalan in 1981 and it would be wonderful to have him again for a cross-cultural ISTA session in India!"

VERSES DOWN THE AGES: *Ranjana Gauhar*

The resplendent phenomenon of classical Odissi of today was not an overnight phenomenon. In the late fifties, a few gurus, alongside

Ranjana Gauhar

a clutch of scholars, took up the handful of movements and gestures practised in the prevalent Gotipua (boys, costumed as girls, dancing in public) and rare Mahari (females dancing inside temples) forms, and sculpted out a style with finesse, — in a concerted effort under 'Jayantika'. Among those pioneers were Kelucharan Mohapatra, Pankaj Charan Das, Debaprasad Das and Mayadhar Raut. And it was the youthful Mayadhar who, having just come out of Chennai's 'Kalakshetra' from under Rukmini Devi Arundale's tutelage, contributed imaginatively in two distinct genres. First, he brought in *Sanchari Bhavas* (elaborations on the basic staple): so liberally used in Bharatanatyam. Second, he contributed new notions in *Abhinaya* (dramatic expression) as embellishments in dance. Both these are standard features in contemporary *Abhinaya* in Odissi Dance.

Sanchari: the Essence of *Abhinaya* in Contemporary Dance was a recent tribute by the Odissi danseuse Ranjana Gauhar to her guru. Says Ranjana, "Mayadhar helped so much in the reshaping, redefining and re-organising Odissi language and vocabulary. Again, his ideas on *Hastamudra Viniyoga* (precepts of hand-gestures) have proved seminal in enriching our repertoire."

Ranjana's innovation is to select poetry spanning a millennium and a half, and to carve her choreography around their variegated themes. She begins with three major *Shlokas* set in *Raga Darbari Kanada* from the celebrated Nandikeshwara treatise 'Abhnaya Darpana' of the late first millennium, — visualising the pure aesthetics of dance; contemplating Shiva as the cosmic dancer with the moon and stars as his adornments; and defining *Patra Lakshana* (character-features) of *Nritya* (interpretative dance). Next comes the nineteenth-century Vidyapati composition in *Raga Kirwani* couched in Maithili: *Woh Sapna Tha…*: as a captivating riddle where Radha describes the attributes of a tree to her Sakhi and asks her to guess the identity of her lover! A Jayadeva *Ashtapadi* (stanza) came next from his lyrical work Gita Govinda: *Rati Sukha Sare Gatam Abhisare…*: in *Raga Yaman* and Ranjana excels especially in her delicate *Chari* (gait) and *Bhramari* (body-rotation).

Oriya poet Kalicharan Pattnaik's recent poem, describing Radha's bemused mind after the departure of Krishna for Mathura and her endless daydreaming about the beloved's return, is evoked beautifully as a Thumri (reminiscent of Bade Ghulam Ali's: *Aye-Na Balam…*) in *Raga Jogia*: using many pensive pauses. The finale was Kalidasa's Ritu Samharam poetry on spring: woven as a melodic bouquet in *Ragas Vasant* (with *Teebra Dhaibat*), *Kafi-Khamaj*, *Bageshri, Malkaunsh* and J*aunpuri*.

Adds Ranjana on her choice of verses, "It's important and even relevant to interpret these exquisite pieces only because they are seldom read these days. They are things of beauty as they capture a multitude of moods and hark back to joyous nature that we seem to be perpetually pushing behind in our material society. Above all, these poems from littérateurs of yore are pregnant with great philosophy, too!"

LANGOURS OF INDOLENT MAIDENS: *Ramli Ibrahim*

Mangalam Bhagavan Vishnu, Mangalam Madhusudanam, / Mangalam Pundarikaksha, Mangalam Garuda Dhwaja... goes the ode to the primordial Divinity of Preservation and, with this, opens the curtains to reveal an opulent stage: With magnificent scenic divides, translucently etched by floral filigree and geometric motifs. Explains Ramli Ibrahim, the director, "They were curvaceous screens to blend with our Odissi and yet portable enough to be packed in a 15-kg bag!" From the dimly lit back emerges the triad of lascivious *Apsaras* (dancers of heaven), soon to be joined by the 'divine-duo': Ramli and Revathi. Happening before the wondering eyes of the devotee (danced with supine grace by Guna), it is a dream come true, when the ancient temple-front springs alive bridging aeons of silence and resonates to the anklet-sounds of the celestial danseuses.

The presentation of *Vision For Ever* by 'Sutra Dance Theatre' from Malaysia is an exotic fare for the cognoscente. Superbly crafted by Ramli using the hoary legacy of Guru Debaprasad Das and his scions, it is Odissi with a difference. Says he, "Our gurus bequeathed us mostly frontal and circular solos. I had re-composed and de-composed them with emphasis on group choreography, — with torsos and backs equally utilised, and enhancing diagonals and spirals with substantial re-designs." The vintage *Mangalacharan,* thus, becomes a delectable carnival of the gods and mortals, and *Hari-Haro* is the powerful composite personification of both Shiva and Vishnu. *Sthayee,* the main pure dance, embellishes multiple verses on iconic sculptures, using *Shilpa Shastra* (treatise on temple architecture), with the sculptor Ramli imparting the aesthetics of positions and postures to disciple Guna.

The standard *Pallavi,* in *Raga Rageshri,* is a virtuoso exposition of *Lasya* – both lyrical and refined – by Ramli and Revathi with an ethereal quality of controlled movement. The melodic *Raga* is personified as a female diva, sired by the love-god Kama and playing

Ramli Ibrahim

veena. *Dasha Mahavidya* is the *piece de resistance*: exploring Debaprasad's involvement in Tantrik traditions to the full and creating ten revelations of the Universal Female – the Goddess Absolute – symbolising, for the awe-struck devotee, Mother Nature in all her physical complexity and intensity. Using virile *Tandavas,* unusual *Mudras* and highly accented *Chowks,* visions were created of her many manifestations: *Kali* (one with blood-thirsty tongue), *Tara, Bhubaneshwari* (benevolent one), *Shodashi* (beauteous 16-year-old one), *Bagala, Chhinnamasta* (one with severed head), *Matangi* (fearsome danseuse), *Bhairavi, Kamala* (wealth-bestowing one) and *Dhoomavati* (smoke-emitting one).

Ramli later teams up with. January to usher in *Ardha Nareeshwara,* — reflecting complimentarity of Shiva with the World Mother Parvati and yet bringing out their opposite polarity. The other dancers, girdling them with silken cloth, are subtly suggestive. The finale is *Moksha,* a pure dance of joy and release, "where we wanted the spectators to join," as Ramli puts it. "Coming from the distant shores of Malaysia with Odissi may not be a disadvantage. With our efforts, quality control and better norms have been achieved for the audience that includes both Indians and local Malayas. Bharatanatyam is more easily available, but it makes a poor second, in terms of standards."

INCANDESCENCE OF ODISSI: *Ileana & Kiran*

Classical Odissi dance — second only to Bharatanatyam in its spread and popularity — was given its structured form and had new items created only in the 1950's, unlike Bharatanatyam which was consolidated many decades earlier by the Tanjavoor Brothers .of Travancore court. Considerable spadework was done by *Jayantika,* the conclave of gurus and scholars; — drawing sculptural resources form the temples and adding initial inspiration from forms like Bharatanatyam for *Mudras* and *Abhinaya.* Three main styles emerged in Odissi from gurus like Pankaj Charan Das, centred on feminine

Maharis, the near-extinct *Devadasis;* Deba Prasad Das rooted in a robust and rustic background, and with *Tantric* touches; and, the most prolific of all, Kelucharan Mohapatra with an instinct for intricate and filigreed treatment both in abstract and expressional aspects. Odissi's fresh inputs come today from the state's research fount-heads like Kala Vikas Kendra; National Music Association; Utkal Sangeet Mahavidyalaya; and Odissi Research Centre.

Kelubabu's legacy is in safe hands, as was evident from the presentation by one of his ace disciples, Ileana Citaristi running her school 'Art Vision' from Bhubaneshwari. Located in the old city and surrounded by numerous temples, she has dedicated herself to evolve a new Odissi choreography, embellished by her earlier European training under the noted thespian, Jerzy Grotoskwy. Explains Ileana, "Kelubabu gave me the most-needed foundation, with emphasis on symmetry and centre-oriented approach. To this, I've added my thought-process on utilisation of space. Since I want my choreography to be suggestive and not linked to the narrative, I copiously use the geometry of space and not necessarily facial or hand-gestures. Elements of movement have their logic: based on fluidity alternating with space-configuration. The aim is to achieve harmony implicit in movement itself." Further, "Grotowsky's accent on total body-movement is more in sync with Seraikela Chhau, coming form the same cultural source as Odissi, which I blend when Odissi needs jumps, show of vigour, even quick flicks of head or neck."

The result was entirely pleasing in the two-day festival amply showcasing new choreography, like *Chitrangada,* looking at the discovery of inner femininity by the Manipuri princess, brought up as a tomboy, at the first body-contact with the virile Arjuna, or, *Saraha,* the Tibetan *Tantric* tale of the learner Saraha, finding the desired master: not in an esoteric guru, but in a low-caste woman who sharpens an arrow-shaft and assumes the totally absorbed posture of aiming the arrow at an invisible target. "The aiming itself is the target, which is the Zen way of looking within," greets Ileana. Her *Tantra,* based on *Saudarya Lahari* and dedicated again to the female energy, was an abstract *Tantric* mould of space-use, while *Ganga-Yamuna* was a descriptive item sourced from Kalidasa's *Raghu Vamsam*, beautifully depicting the two rivers as different strings of blue sapphire and white pearls strung together, or, as the black and white swans directing themselves to lake Mansarovar.

The Uday Shankar Festival saw Kiran Sehgal presenting three choreographic pieces, using the grammar of Odissi dance. Her approach was radically different, as she declares, "I don't have any pre-set design, but follow the dictates of my creative instinct, to keep adding or removing gestures and movements till they come to a cohesive whole. Choreography to me is a total amalgam of sense of space, layout, design and balance. My nonagenarian mother, Zohra Sehgal, keeps commenting that I've inherited – for my contemplative works — the genes from my father Kameshwar who, together with my mother, ran 'Zoresh Centre' in Lahore and later, 'Sehgal Ballet Troupe' in Mumbai. To me, choreography has been an organic process, comprising painting, display and design, sketching and drawing: the disciplines that I grew with at the Ealing School of Art and St. Martin School of design, both in London."

In *Whispering Mood,* Kiran used L Subramanian's music, to allow her dancers express a feeling for melody at different moments of time. *Agni: the Fire Within* was a more complex piece with veiled women who were suppressed, and suffered regardless of their identity. Avers Kiran, "Despite India having a woman PM, a woman President and as many as four women CMs (now changed) at present, women are subject of feticide and infanticide, and undergo traumatic brutalisation, begging constantly for justice." In *Talangya,* seven dancers moved like kinetic sculpture, making a mighty wavc of energy break into whirlpools of tiny energy. An ancient Dhrupad *dhun* provided the musical staple, with percussion ensemble of Mardala, Tabla, Hindustani Pakhawaj, Mridangam, Khol, Manjira and big Nagara. The tempo built up from very slow to a tumultuous crescendo at the end. No wonder, Kiran says, "It takes my whole energy and I get totally drained when I finish my composition!"

WHEN ODISSI WENT WEST: *Sudha Grover*

They were fourteen bright young things with luminous eyes and, barring one, were in India – New Delhi, Agra, Balasore and Bhuvaneswar — for their very first performance, having come from across half the globe! Settled in New Jersey, USA, they were from 'Sudhamini Dance Academy' under Sudha Grover, a teacher of 30 years' standing under Guru Hare Krishna Behera. Falling between the ages 13 to 20 and dancing Odissi, they and their teacher had one point in common: none of them belonged to Orissa.

"When I went to the USA in the seventies, there was no Odissi dancer there and I was probably the first person to start an Odissi teaching centre for kids from 5 upwards," ruminates Sudha. "Now

Sudha Grover's Group

there're centres in California and Connecticut, beside Michigan and Pittsburgh. All told, there would be 10-12 Odissi centres in the West: nowhere comparable to the scores of Bharatanatyam institutions." Being second-generation Americans preoccupied in Western life, why should they hark back to such classical dance styles? Responds Sudha, "Regardless of their parental pressures, they themselves are mature enough these days to look for their roots and try to imbibe an Indian value system, to the extent feasible, even compromising their busy hours. This also is the precise reason why the white community is today open to enjoying our dances, but not ready to learn them, as they don't connect to them."

Adds she, "Not many Odissi gurus visit the USA, but teachers from there keep coming back to India: to pick up what is new. Mostly young performers go there, except once for the Odissi gathering in Washington, when many gurus turned up. On my part, I've been coming back every year." On choice between solo and group-productions abroad, "Group-choreography can accommodate more dancers and capture vivid attention. While the solo needs hard work for perfection, it's sustaining interest-level is limited. Youngsters love dancing in groups, although it takes long to learn perfect synchronisation in group-choreography. In teaching, of course, one-to-one correspondence is important."

Most of the group items are a treat to the eye. *Mangalacharan* built upon Adi Shamkar's *Bhawani Ashtakam* and eulogising Shakti: as embodiment of power and valour. It is delightfully choreographed. The *piece de resistance* is *Dashavatar,* with all fourteen girls orchestrating myriad movements both to presage and to present the ten Vishnu incarnations down the evolutionary line. Very strikingly costumed — in contrasting black and white shades and stripes – they create a rare chiaroscuro on the stage. The other arresting item is the final *Moksha* evoking many shades of energetic hues and patterns. The balance items could possibly do with more of *Anga Shuddhi* (body discipline), but undoubtedly it would come in time.

"They arrived only seven days back and guru-*ji* corrected their postures and enhanced the choreographic structure," points out Sudha. "I've brought them here not merely to hone their skills, but to acquaint them with such heritage as Konarak sun-temple. Music, language and religion are necessary for them to imbibe beside dance. Instead of separate teaching, we encourage open interactions. You'll be surprised on the number of questions they ask: relating to our legacy and tradition, our myths and legends. A lively, insatiate mind is half the battle won for such teenagers."

REMEMBERING GURU PANKAJ CHARAN: *Ratna Roy*

It was an Odissi performance with a difference. Built around the considerable repertoire of Guru Pankaj Charan Das – who died in 2004 – it was designed as an ode to the late guru and attempted to bring out his extraordinary prowess in choreography. The Odissi danseuse Ratna Roy who came from the USA for this purpose, presented, beside herself, her considerably-talented 'mixed-blood' disciples: Scheherazaad Cooper and Sitara Thobani, along with Chapala Misra from Puri, heading the performance.

Ratna Roy

Cooper hits off with a *Mangalacharan* on *Navadurga*, followed by a *Mahari-Suchi-Sringara* by Thobani, and then both the dancers perform *Shankarabharanam Pallavi* with great élan. Ratna's own item: *Kuru Yadunandana* was the *piece de resistance* of the evening. An *Ashtapadi* from *Gita Govinda*, it has been seen enacted by the great Guru Kelu Charan Mahapatra several times, but Ratna brings out a unique blend of the spiritual and the sensual, using her underplayed expressions. While the next *Vasanta Pallavi* is done by Chapala, the finale is *Draupadi* from Ratna's successful repertoire *Pancha Kanya*, on the five much-maligned women from the epics. All thirteen stalwarts of the Kaurava court and Draupadi's futile appeals to their better selves are etched with distinctive to-and-fro movements and very differently-nuanced approaches to the five Pandavas, her last resort.

Describing Pankaj Charan as the only one among the Odissi masters who was actually the son of a Devadasi, Ratna recalls, "He grew up in a matrilineal tradition and imbibed strong female-centred ethos. It is interesting that he was the guru of Kelu Charan at Annapurna-B theatre for two years and was the choreographer of *Dasavatara*, the first ever classical Odissi dance, with music composed by Durga Charan Durlabh and danced by Kelu Charan and Lakshmipriya (later Kelu Charan's wife). Pankaj Charan's grip on the feminine *Mahari ang* was, therefore, supreme. To depict *Lasya*, he makes the upper torso of the dancer subtly separated from the lower body's footwork. Next, there is a remarkable 'punctuation' of the hip, in that the hip is meant to be there but not visible, with torso movement decidedly looking slow. Third, a piece like *Kuru Yadunandana* would use *Abhanga* (no body-bend): with feet firmly together, hip out and glances showing circular movement (unlike Kelubabu's eyes going from side-to-side without dropping). Fourth, eyes should always acknowledge deity and royalty. Fifth, there would be a special *Kara Bhramari* (hand circularity), not used by other gurus. Finally, for an item like *Shankarabharanam Pallavi*, torso movement can be circular, — horizontally, vertically or side-to-side."

Coming to *Abhinaya*, Ratna adds, "All guru-ji's dances veer between spirituality and sensuality, — with a dancer being alternately Lord God and devadasi. Especially for *Gita Govinda*, he opined that since Radha was not married to Krishna and, therefore, not possessed by him, Radha's character is very strong and should be shown as such. His *Abhinaya* was to be viewed from a female perspective and, in an 18-minute dance-drama, he would devote forty seconds to dice. When two men played dice, what happened out of it that viscerally affected a woman like Draupadi? Further, his choreography was largely taken from the life in Puri, such as, *Shringara* of *Mahari ang* and *Medho Nacha* during the Puri Shahi Yatra festival, when each actor would don an independent role with a halo behind the head, made of solapith. Again, there was what I call 'dialogic choreography' where spirituality would come out of a constant dialogue among the performer's mind, performer's body and the choreographer. Even when I use footwork, the bringing out of *Abhinaya* would remain most important."

Holding the chair on dance at Evergreen State College in Olympia and having researched into the African-American literature, has she used her Odissi knowledge in any blended form? "Yes, I have blacks among the foremost of classical Odissi dancers in my 'Urvashi' group. When I was commissioned to choreograph *Broken Dreams* to commemorate Martin Luther King Day in January 2000, I used two black dancers to enact King and Malcolm X, and eight white dancers to form a crowd. I made the latter recapitulate, on paper, as to why they wanted ever to lynch the black and used their bias to frame threatening advances, against the fragmented utterances of King: *I have a dream*... Their body language came from my Odissi repertoire!"

POP ART OF PUPPETRY: *Shagun Butani, Anurupa Roy*

It is all about the magic blue / Vishnu and his celestial hue / Whenever in the world / Evil was a lot / And good was not / Vishnu who is God / Made a plot / And used his hue / To colour a chosen few … Thus ran the jingle as the leit motif of the entire show. Inspired by the abiding Krishna mythology, *Magic Blue* was brought by thirteen children in the age group of 7-12, hand-in-hand with seasoned puppeteers: to take on the enthralled viewers through the wondrous world of men, gods and demons, in a breath-taking, interactive puppet-human spectacle.

The tone is set by a quick-fire *Dashavatar* in a topsy-turvy array of Vishnu's first few incarnations: with the 'shadow' cut-outs of fish, tortoise, boar and Narasimha all peeping through the illumined, coloured screen and kids romping around: in sync with the stylised images flashing in the rear. Then come Krishna and his adversarial serpent-demon *Kaliya* as the larger-than-life composite puppets of fiery, sinewy kind in 'black lamp': glowing in white-and-velvet, rather than in the conventional black hue. The demon *Bakasur* is a pre-historic figure made of reptilian features: with monstrous pink beaks, white-foam wings and a body of – hold your breath! – washing-machine tubes. It does not make a whit of difference in credibility, — when the creature comes flapping over the balcony above, or, suddenly leaps from behind the stage-curtains. The other demon *Aghasur* is an amalgam of frothy clouds of bubble-wrap, finally collapsing on the stage as an amorphous mass. The *piece de resistance* is the ten-foot puppet-Kamsa – the humanoid demon, manipulated by four black-veiled puppeteers in imitative Bunraku style – confronting a trio of highly agile, four-foot Krishnas. The gusto and bravado with which the little dancers fight all the four demons is absolutely infectious; obviously children frightfully enjoy killing demons!

Magic Blue

Says the petite choreographer Shagun Butani, who was also the scriptwriter; “My children have all learnt Odissi for at least two years, besides Seraikela Chhau and elements of modern dance. Combining even basic dance-steps and gestures with large puppets and mystifying masks was a little surreal, but children grew wonderfully into the interaction — of gods, demons and men! Shyam Banerji’s music, composed after the movements and choreography were all conceptualised, jelling really well, as sung by his 7-year old niece! My three senior students did the triple Krishna: weaving many choreographic patterns in the typical *Raas Lila* manner.”

Endorses Anurupa Roy, the seasoned puppet-director, “We took rather long to first visualise the scenario, and then design the storyboard and create the actual puppets. But, in practice, rehearsals took only three months. We did take a lot of creative liberty: in using bubble-wrap material for the scenography. We adopted, on the whole, a pop-art approach: to create comic-book characters in puppetry: as though the whole *Amar Chitra Katha* would come alive!” On the whole, it was liberation of imagination and worked remarkably well!

Kathak

Saswati Sen

Overview

Light and Dark Shades of This Progressive Era

by Saswati Sen

When I stated learning Kathak more than two decades ago, it was difficult to convince my friends, my feelings of joy and satisfaction, my passion for learning, —— how I could forgo all other entertainments and fun against my classes. There were no stage performances or TV appearances to look forward to, but somehow learning was joy. When I had my first solo programme, I had a sound training of nearly 12-13 years. The audience was not so trained, — just about 30%-40% people knew about the details of Kathak. Probably, the period between the middle 50's to early 70's was a big struggling period and less eventful in the Kathak scenario.

Gradually the solo form began to be replaced by group work and dance-dramas or thematic presentations. Audiences started taking interest as the common masses could understand better. Pt. Birju Maharaj and Smt. Kumudini Lakhia were two pioneers in bringing about great changes in the content and presentation. From thematic, the focus shifted to abstract choreography, which enhanced the visual appeal. By this time, the audiences were ready to accept, as they understood the form and its strength. From the mid-70's until the end-90's was probably the best time when Kathak grew in its group of choreographic work. However, the focus and beauty of the solo form was getting lost.

Gradually, Kathak dancers shifted their focus to choreography, which has become the biggest disaster in the last 10-12 years. Every work is a copy of something done before; and the strength of the form is lost to lighting and stage- gimmicks. However, the realisation has started showing up, and again in the recent past (about 2-3 years), the dancers are becoming conscious of the importance of real art. The need today is to focus on good training and sincere, dedicated hard work to regain the depth of the divine form.

THE FAMILY CONFLUENCE: *Birju Maharaj*

The Capital's entire art cognoscente converged into the hall whose gates were locked long before the show began. The cause for celebration was not just that February 3 was Pt. Birju Maharaj's 70th birthday but that all three generations of his family were going to perform together for the first time. Doing justice to the Delhite's belief that the invigorating juice of dance ran in their veins thicker than the blood, the evening put Maharaj-*ji* to head the illustrious list of performers, — to be followed by Ram Mohan Maharaj and Krishan Mohan Maharaj, the scions of his dear departed uncle Shambhu Maharaj who once reigned in Kathak with unparalleled prowess for *Abhinaya.* After Maharaj-*ji's* own generation would come his sons: Jai Kishan Maharaj and Deepak Maharaj and the only dancing daughter (the two others, Kavita and Anita, having married and having left the family's vocation): Mamta Maharaj. Then would come Ipshita Mishra, the granddaughter of Shambhu, and – crowning the list – would appear the three talented grandchildren of Maharaj-*ji:* Ragini Mishra, daughter of Deepak; Tribubhan Maharaj, son of Jai Kishan; and the two-something Sinjini Kulkarni, Anita's sweet darling!

Birju Maharaj

Adds Saswati who arranged the brilliant confluence, "You must remember that the family-tree went back deep into the history of UP's story-telling 'Kathakars' or 'Kathaks', and Maharaj-*ji* is the seventh generation. His great grandfather was Daya Prasad, the nascent court-dancer for the royalty of Oudh, and grandfather Binda Din was the reigning dancer-composer-choreographer of the court of his time, — with countless Thumris bequeathed by him to posterity. Binda Din had three sons: Maharaj-*ji's* father Achchan Mahharaj; Shambhu and the youngest Lachchu Maharaj, with mastery in *Layakari* and *Lasya,* — nicknamed 'Lachchu' because of his proclivity for Mumbai's lascivious celluloid world! He left no children."

Maharaj-ji, visibly humbled by the overwhelming audience response, chips in, "I was a mere Brijnarayan Prasad Mishra. Your affection has made me Birju-Bhai, Birju-Chacha and Birju Maharaj. Basically I'm a painter who has sought your support and continued to etch his life's creations in as many colours as possible. But I've only scratched the surface of our great arts and have as much a feeling of inadequacy as had my father who — asked why he confined himself so much to *Teentaal* and seldom went beyond — replied: 'I haven't fully learnt even *Teentaal*; how can I go to other rhythms?' I, too, have only one lifetime for my art. It's much like a malleable piece of iron and it depends how you use it or abuse it." He recites his own poem then, "*The iron-piece lay there abjectly neglected. Then came the ironsmith who heated it up and hammered out of it a shining sword that the soldiers took away to kill men. But when the sculptor arrived, he moulded out of it a temple-bell whose vibrant rings could be heard far and wide by the devout men!*"

The show began at the tender end when Ragini and Tribubhan, already looking like finished artists, executed an expert *Teentaal*. And then sauntered in Sinjini, the tiny tot, whose mere walk to the centre-stage was given a rousing ovation, as if it was symbolic of the shape of things to come! Says a pert Ragini, who is in the 4th grade, "I think I'll take up dancing only as a hobby and keep it as such alongside studies." Ipshita followed with a Thumri: *Raina Badaria* in *Teentaal*, with a very pleasant face and quicksilver steps, to win the viewers' hearts. Explains a confident Ipshita, "I've just completed my graduation in Computer Sciences, but that has become irrelevant, now that I've decided to make Kathak my career. No, I'm not dancing due to family pressure, but out of my own choice. Indeed, my endeavour would be to maintain the family tradition."

In the generation next, there was no doubt that the heritage was in good hands. Deepak, for instance, chose – instead of *Teentaal* – a most unusual *Panch Sawari* with 15-beats. A slim, winsome stage-personality, he turned out to be a very sensitive dancer, showing the rhythmic skills on a tightrope walk. Rightly called a 'shining star' of the art scene, he kept the audience spellbound. Says a modest Deepak, "What I concentrate upon is a '*Taalgunjan*' with a synergy of *Bandish, Taal*, and my whole body, and present *Upajs* (creative pieces). I've today two huge canvases before me: Classical tradition on one side and the modernity on the other, both beckoning me. I've to tread on my path carefully and rise up to my own ability..."

The elder brother Jaikishan chose a 4-line *Bandish* of Dhrupad in *Raga Vasant*, which he had composed himself and had Deepak – already an established singer as well — as his vocal support. A veteran of many concert tours abroad, having performed solo and group compositions with his father, Jaikishan enhanced his reputation in creativity in all areas of music composition, drumming and choreography, when he moved into *Ginti-Ka Tihai*, playing on permutation of rhythmic beats. "My idea to deal with such *Tihais* is to make rhythms accessible to the common man used to counting." With Deepak in the wings, he launched a Thumri: *Umara Jhumara Raasa Ragahao* ...

Then came the sister Mamata, incidentally the first female Kathak performer in the family, — otherwise boasting of a great lineage of male artists. Her choice was a *Dhamar Taal* for a composition: *Jalata Awata Hai, Kah Do Sabaria Ko*... in *raga Bharavi.* The audience loved it, and obviously she has carved out a niche for herself. The only point of caution for both her and for Jaikishan would be to watch out on their girth-line, as excessive avoirdupois would be a killer-factor for any dancer who must regard the body as the only tool for art.

Next in line was guru Shambhu's legacy. The point that unmistakably emerged was the intricate artistry that he could weave on the sheer gait of *Gat Nikas*. Ram Mohan, who took the stage with Deepak again at the helm for music and *Padhant*, is among the leading dancers of his generation. He evinced the style of expression acquired from his father and exuded grace and finesse acquired from the family. Said he, "I'd do some old and some new concepts. It's a moment of my greatest joy that our whole family has congregated here for performance and shares our skills." About the nature of accompaniment he emphasises, "We didn't get together earlier, but met only here." The role of improvisation was, unlike the set and pre-rehearsed formats of other classical dances, refreshingly evident in the performance of what could be called the 'first family of Kathak' in the land. He executed *Gat Nikas* with five forms of *Ghunghats* — in which at least one *Sakhi* bites on her veil and simultaneously tries to peep out – and brought the house down. Coming to Thumri, he admits, "When Dad taught Uma Sharma, I used to watch furtively and later copied her: colyrium and all. Maharaj-*ji* has achieved a *Sangam* of all three maestros and made it available to us." Terming *Ginti–ke Tihai* as primarily counting and as vital as life, he switched over to a family Thumri: *Hatho Chhero Na*…

Krishna Mohan, the elder brother and perhaps the best torchbearer of Shambhu's *Gharana*, has a slim figure and a masculine bearing, which a Mexican critic, Dr. Agnes Victoria, mesmerised by the evening, termed 'very fit and virile, with subtlest of energy.' He confesses, "Allahabad has just seen the end of baths at the end of the 3-day 'Kumbha Mela' and here I've come for bathing in 'Kathak Kumbha'! Initiation from Dad in older traditions has seen vigorous renovations in Maharj-ji's hands and, although all of 52 years, I feel small in front of other stalwarts." Belying his humility, he launched some traditional *Teentaal*, – with *Padhant* provided impromptu by Saswati from the wings — and some scintillating *Gat Nikas* and an enchanting Thumri; *Khelo Holi Re Kanhaiya*… He too supports improvisation to the hilt: "I come without rehearsals and try to make my solo always independent and always uninhibited!" He demonstrated it best by making the packed gathering give claps and dancing to their varied beats, again and again, — with Saswati swirling in from the wings and doing exciting pirouettes as *Pas de Deux*!

The place of honour, kept apart for Maharaj-*ji*, saw him take over the reins and show the best of improvisation, by inviting Rajan-Sajan Mishra brother-duo onto the stage and weaving an on-the-spot *Gat Bhav* and *Gat Nikas* to their Thumri: *Mori Tori, Tori Mori, Na Banegi Shyam*.. His breath-taking repertoire ranged from the subdued silence of *Ghungroos* (anklets); *Nayak-Nayika-Samvad* with the two feet talking different lines for the love-besotted couple; the *Tehais* to establish the four cardinal directions; the pair of parrot and swan; the duality of tabla-pair; and the dialogue of the lazy and the hyperactive. Points out Maharaj-*ji*, "I'm very alive to the all-abiding rhythm in Nature: waves of oceans, sweeps of the winds, even the moving human fingers on sitar. Have you seen the busy clerk noting on the office-file, — does he not remind you of rhythm?"

The finale came thundering with yet another — and really grand — improvisation. Maharaj-*ji* invited all the four *tabaliyas* of the evening: Govinda Chakravarty, Ambika Prasad Mishra, Debashis Mukherjee and Manoj Srivastava to play to his instantly made-out *Tehais*. As though it were not enough, the four uncles and nephews joined him: Krishna Mohan and Ram Mohan, joining hands with Jaikishan and Deepak. and weaving neat footwork: solo and together. Concludes Maharaj-ji, "Kalashram has given my whole family space for self-expression and I'm beholden to Saswati and her compatriots for allowing the unique experiment to happen!"

ONLY AFTER FOUR DECADES: *Munnalal Shukla*

The evening belonged to Guru Munna Shukla and splendours of the rich Kalka-Bindadin tradition of Lucknow *Gharana* of Kathak, which

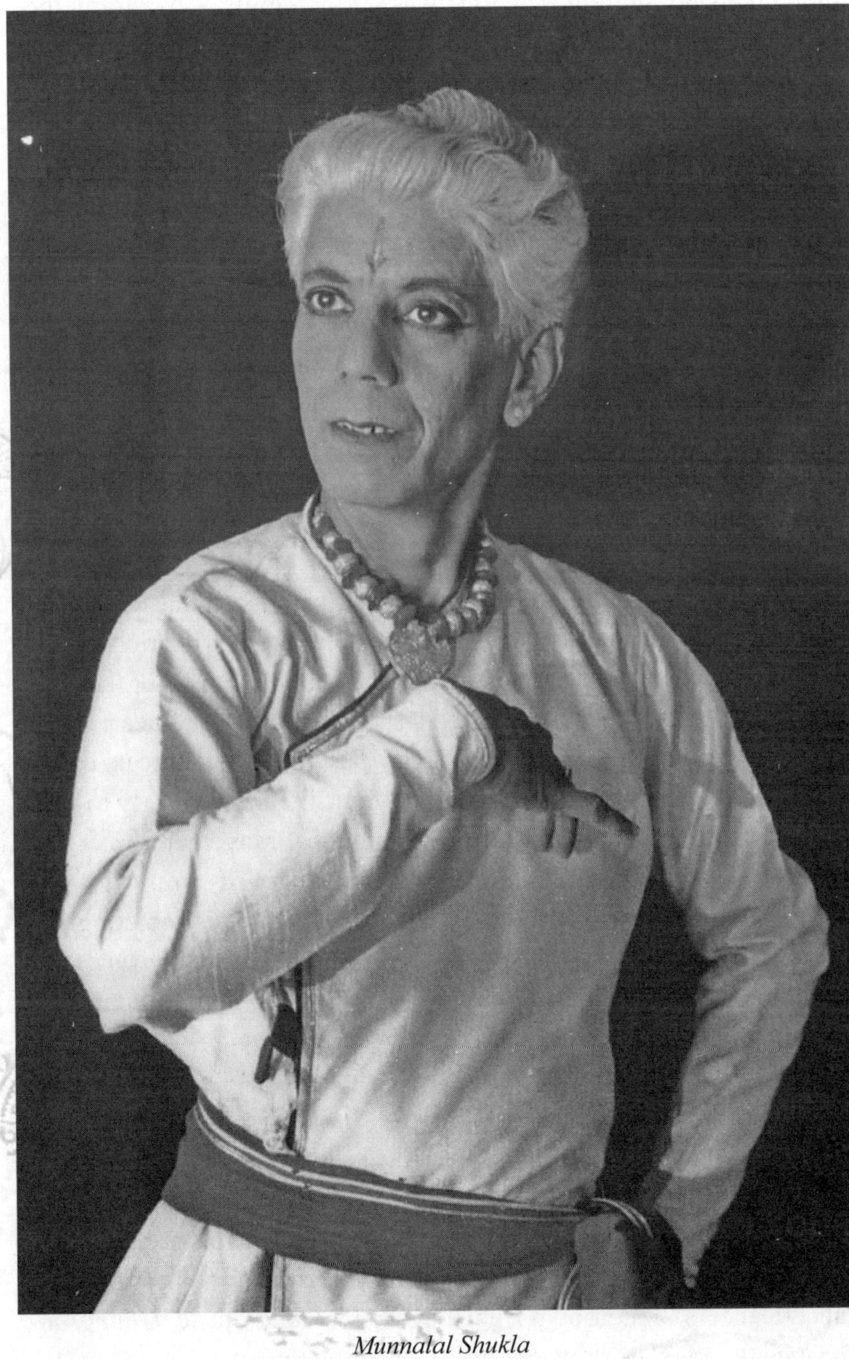

Munnalal Shukla

coloured his upbringing. The tone was set by Sumitra Charatram, the nonagenarian art-activist, who whispers, "He is the son of Shambhu Maharaj's sister. You see, when I started Shriram Bharatiya Kala Kendra as a young woman, I wanted to revive Kathak, which was then considered prostitutes' art. So I had Shambhu Maharaj, already a legendary artist, from Lucknow *Gharana;* Sunder Prasad from Jaipur *Gharana;* and the celebrated Siddheswari Devi from Banaras *Gharna* for vocal support. Munna was among our first students, besides Kumudini Lakhia and Uma Sharma. I'm happy that their kind of excellence could be held as our current hallmark!" Readily admits Munna, "It was to SBKK and Sumitra-*ji* that I owe my training and track-record. I have no regrets that I'm performing on a public platform today after an unbelievable gap of 40 years! In this interregnum, I've tried not to deviate from my true self."

The evening proved him to be right. As an established master – in Kathak and then outside – he has been known for his rich vocabulary, intricate *Layakari* and nuanced expressions. For the current demonstrations, he selected a sequence that was linear: *Alap, Jod, Jhala* and used some extraordinary *Bandishes* set in beats of seven and a quarter, or, eight and three-fourth! His sensitivity to the aesthetics of visual images and dynamics of movement was remarkable, coupled with the chosen intricacies of rhythm. After some initial *Padhants* for *Uthan, Thaat* and *Gat Nikas,* depicting innovative *Layakari,* he switched over to *Natabari* and *Bansuri*, revealing many unexpected turns in their interpretation. His dance rendering of a *Dhrupad* by Dagar brothers: *Kunjana Me Racho Raas....:* in *Raga Khamaj,* was most alluring. After playing with some hidden *Sams* and *Go-Puchcha* (cow-tail) *Bandishes,* he concluded with a scintillating *Tehai.*

The rest of the evening belonged to his disciples: Jayashree, Susmita, Deepti and Nisha: all accomplished dancers, choreographers and dance-teachers in their own rights. Set to recorded music, *Ghungroo Tarang* attempted to show evolution of music through *Tatkars* and

Tukras in different *Jatis.* Silence too had a resonance, which came pulsating alive with dexterous usage of varied tonal emphases of the foot. Out of the emerging silence came *Tarang:* described as "the willful flow of ocean-waves as they dip and rise playfully in an effort to reach the seashore." Endorses Munna, "*Tarang* comprises also the rhythmic patterns reaching out to meet their own shore — the *Sam*! "

Chaturang, as the finale, had a novel approach, attempting to mirror Hindustani classical music by taking its components: *Khayal* (word-patterns), *Tirvat* (mnemonic-patterns), *Sargam* (note-patterns) and *Tarana* (blending words and mnemonics). Instead of a single *Raga* and *Tala,* Ustad Yusuf Khan's music chose a whole garland of them. Thus, a *Lakshana Geet* set it off with *Raga Marwa* and *Tala Dhamar;* followed by *Khayal* in *Raga Basant* and *Tala Jhaptal; Tirvat* in *Raga Basant Bahar* and *Tala Rupak; Sargam* in *Raga Bahar* and *Tala ektal;* and *Tarana* in *Raga Kaushik Dhuni* and *Tala Teental.* Munna's classical choreography for his quartet of danseuses was simply exhilarating!

BRAVURA AND THE EPHEMERA: *Shovana Narayan*

Rebel, freedom fighter, patriot, radical activist, storywriter and documentary filmmaker, Ali Sardar Jafri has been all this at once. As one of the seven founders of the Progressive Writers Movement in Lucknow, he was in the vanguard of Indian literati since the 1930's. But, above all, he was a poet endowed with rare sensibility and regarded as one of the brightest stars in the 20th century Urdu poetry firmament. In *Mera Safar,* his celebrated *Nazma,* he declared himself to be immortal, as he would live eternally in the sweet song of birds and smile of dry leaves. Even after death, he would remain alive so long as crops dance in the fields. Much like Ghalib, he too believed that one day all the golden rivers and blue lakes in the sky would reverberate with the music of his being…

Shovana Narayan

Mera Safar, in its incarnation as Kathak ballet by Shovana Narayan and the adornment of paintings by Serbjeet Singh of Gaumukh and other visions of the Himalayas, was not the dancer's first love affair with that *Nazma.* Shovana had it showcased first in 1991 with the poet himself chanting the lines. But her *Amour Propre* began much earlier, as she vividly recalls, "I met his son with 'Uncle' and 'Auntie' in Mumbai in 1971. Afterwards, whenever we were in the same town, we'd meet, but they were by then 'Bhaiya' and 'Bhavi'! I knew he shot into fame being a nationalist, but his philosophical bend was always universal. Indeed, he'd translated Ghalib's ode to Banaras, *Charagh-e-Dai,* to which I danced in the early 1990's. There Banaras is declared as 'Kaba' of the entire Hindustan, — to all communities. Simultaneously, he was – as in *Abla-Pa* – a born *Musafir: Kis des-se Aya Tha, Kis Des-me Jana Hai...*"

Shovana begins *Mera Safar* in frenzy, where her dance has a sense of intoxication, eyed by appreciative students and the cognoscente. "Then there's a thud, life gets over and the candle-flame goes off. My eyes close, my spirit withers away." declares the danseuse. She echoes the poet: *All the forms / Flowering like buds / And smiling like flowers will be lost / And the beating of the heart / Will go to slumber...And then no one will ask / 'Where is Sardar in the assembly?'* ...

The littlest of the children (Madhavi) comes and the apparently dejected Shovana opens her eyes. For, *I will return here again and again. / I will speak with the lips of the children. / I will sing with the throats of birds. // When seeds will smile in the womb of creation, / And young shoots, with their fingers, / Will tickle the layers of earth. / Then from leaf to leaf and bud to bud, / I will open my eyes again...*

There are paeans of laughter of youngsters and blossoms of her yard, before autumn strikes: *When the winter winds will blow / the stark autumn to the world, / The sound of my laugher will be heard. / From the dry crunch of leaves, / Under the tread of youthful feet...*

Till then, *Harek Ashiq Hai Sardar Yahan, Harek Mashuq Sultana Hai* ..."Why am I so scared?" asks she. "For a fleeting moment, my whole future passes me by. Students come then with an *Ati Vilambit 'Dha'* and the footwork goes from *Duguna* to *Chowguna* around me*: Main Sota Hun, Main Jagta Hun / Jag-ke Fir-se So Jata Hun / Sadiyon-ka Purana Khoya-hun Main / Mar-ke Amar Ho Jata Hun*...It is the sojourn of essence, to transience, back to essence.

Adds Shovana on Serbjeet Singh's parallel evocation, "His Himalayas in 1991 showed me the up-and-down of life and his glistening rivers contained the swift flow of energy. I found them resonant to Sardar Jafri's theme!"

OF STEREOTYPES AND ARCHETYPES:
Shovana & Aditi

Is the classical genre of Kathak falling into a groove? While the storytelling in Kathak has been relegated to the past, most dancers (not all) carry on the stereotype of standing front-stage and launching a virtual diatribe, — to explain steps and perform them individually. This mannerism, which Kathak artists insist in calling "Traditional Kathak", was amusingly named by Pt. Ravi Shankar as "lecture-demonstration," treating the assembled audience as a gathering of students! Since other classical dancers have long discarded such overtures and proceed to present items right away once on stage, does Kathak need to maintain their stereotype?

Shovana Narayan, the celebrated Kathak danseuse, vehemently challenges the accusation, "It's not 'lec-dem' by any means, but an essential adjunct of presentation, with a beauty of its own. It's basically an exploration of the entire dance-canvas and aesthetics of the rhythm-world, conjuring up Kathak's entire life-cycle that dates back to antiquity. It was the dance of the Indo-Gangetic belt and the earliest group of Kathak dancers is convincingly documented to be from Banaras in the 4th century BC, finding ample references in the *Mahabharata.* It's a whole tradition with so much possibility."

After a dramatic *Manch Pravesh* (stage-entry) and an invocation: *Vande Vishnu Bhava-Bhaya Haranam...,* she showed some dazzling footwork, and the skirt-lifting re-created the ambience of aristocratic gatherings of yore. Images of the dancing gods: Hara with *damaru* (small drum) and Hari with flute: accompanied by *mridanga* (big drum) came through vividly. Then came patterns of movements and gestures — with even leaps of the tadpole – adding *Abhinaya* (expressions) of thunders, lightning and the rains. After a conventional *Chira Haranam* (garment-stealing) episode of Draupadi, the best piece was the trials and travails of contemporary woman from a popular Bhojpuri poem: *Sakhi Re, Kaison Badalal Jiwanawa Re...,* set to tune by Mahesh Prasad. The anguish of the eternally toiling, grain-pounding, child-suckling femininity ended with a glimmer of hope and a dream in the eyes.

If Shovana was the archangel of Kathak stereotype, Aditi Mangaldas came through as the queen of its archetypes, — throwing in original models and prototypes. Her opening item was *Through Meerabai* with the love-smitten song: *Ramaiya, Main To Thaare Rang Rati...* Without any divertissement, she let loose her quick-silver movements, astonishing jumps, strong pirouettes and occasional misty-eyed dreams in rock-still postures, — setting the stage ablaze. It was Meera's defiance of the world, the utter abandon of an intoxicated being overwhelmed by her *amour propre: I gaze, amazed at your beauty. I am engulfed in your love and drenched with your colours! O beloved, my eyes are wonderstruck. Your body glows with the adornment jewels. Each limb glistens with lustre and brilliance! I've become one with you...*

The other piece was *Through Hazrat Amir Khusrau: Chashme-Masti Ae Jabeen, Zulfe-Daraazi Ae Jabeen...* She contorted and convoluted with the Sufiana Kalam: *O wondrous eyes full of piety, O wondrous tresses wavy and long, O wondrous wine-worshipper, O wondrous mischievous one*...If the earlier piece was flamboyant; the latter one was languorous to the core. Expatiates Aditi, "I found Meera's and Khusrau's sentiments singularly similar! While I fleshed out Meera's express abnegations and yet contentment that she was coloured in His colours, Khusrau's was imbued with subtle spirituality. I brought in suggestions of the Dervish's dance, yet I filled up my dance-space with *Padhant, Tukra, Chakkar, Gat Nikas.* In other words, mine was Kathak-spinning with a Sufi touch, but also mingled with flourishes from Rajasthan's *Kalbeliya* and *Teraatali* forms: with my fingers beseeching sound from my *ghungroos* (anklets). On the whole, I'm exploring textures, while my themes become numinous with feelings of trance!"

EXPLORING THE INFINITE: *Aditi Mangaldas*

Are there fixed goals in life? We do map out our sojourn on this planet earth in terms of milestones and cherished dreams, but can we keep them up in time? Hasn't the philosopher Krishnamurti violently negated the notion: *We look for the fixed points, but there are none, either in ourselves or outside in the universe; To live without these fixed points is our challenge*.... Aditi Mangaldas, coming from among the deep-thinking fraternity, takes the question farther, "What lies beyond the realm of the known, beyond what our mind can perceive, as hidden in the deep recesses of our heart?"

Aditi Mangaldas' s Group

Uncharted Seas by Aditi, premiered by 'Natya Ballet Centre', is like a chimera in light-and-shade that conducts a search – physical, emotional, psychological – into the realms of the unknown. It uses all the tenets of Kathak: *Abhinaya,* technical wizardry, space, ambience: building up its composition in fantasy through a melodic space that builds up *laya* from *Ati Vilambit, Vilambit, Madhya, Drut* to *Ati Drut.* In fact, the music – lusciously woven by Shubha Mudgal, with tabla support by Aneesh Pradhan – is throughout in *Raga Bageshri* that leaves out the stable notes of *Rishav* and *Dhaivat* in the ascent and imparts a tension that pervades the ballet throughout with articulating of *Sargam.*

The choreography remains a rare treat. First, there are the corridors of light for the external search in the enveloping darkness: with lamps in hand, and faces half-turned or averted. *You will find freedom, truth, beauty, love, which are one and the same, only when you no longer seek them...,* Aditi quotes Krishnamurti and then Bharatendu Harishchandra: *Let it be revealed to these eyes that are thirsty....* The energetic solo catches the Meera bhajan's refrain of the evanescent beauty in the abstract: *Main to Tharo Rangrati...* Dancing damsels emerge from the nothingness of dark to look at beauty that is now amazingly effulgent: executing *Gat Nikas* with gentle footfalls in slow *Tihais*, for the manifestation, a la Malihabadi: *...like the soft sound of a dewdrop falling upon a leaf in a dream.*

Then comes the raging storm and Aditi recapitulates Rumi: *My heart is on fire, / in my madness I roam the desert, / The flames of my passion / devour the wind and the sky....* There is a brilliant Kathak piece to the tune of Kabir: *Is Me Chanda, Is Me Sur / Is Ghata Gaaze Anahata Tur...* for the gaze within. The finale comes when the entire search ends and the quest shows now radiant dancers with lit-up lamps again. Muses Aditi, "All that one seeks is there, and if one is silent, without outward or inward movement, then it is revealed."

Adds she, “Plato said somewhere that it’s a failure if one form of art can be translated into another; it has to be transformation. We’ve attempted even a transcreation: from meditations and melodies, choreography and cadences: where all members have given of their best and a wonderful rapport is achieved in the process. And we’ve always remembered David Bohm: *The field of the finite is all that we can see, hear, touch, remember and describe. This field is basically that which is manifest or tangible. The essential quality of the infinite, by contrast, is its subtlety, its intangibility...”*

A KALEIDO SCOPE OF KATHAK: *Drishtikon*

The on-going changes in Kathak style – the pride of the Northern Hindi belt from Jaipur to Lucknow, with sinews running up to Banaras and Raipur — have been seminal, inside of a single generation. The genre has grown far away from its genesis where it morphed village storytellers, ‘Kathaks’ or ‘Kathakars’, into dancers, — having completely shed now the ‘Kathavachan’ character. In the lifetime of one luminary, Pt. Birju Maharaj, whose forefathers danced primarily solo items at royal courts, one notices at least three quantum changes: Maharaj-ji as dance-partner of Kumudini Lakhia in India and Overseas, and imbibing *pas-de-deux* sensibilities from the West; as master-choreographer for dance-dramas like *Shan-e-Oudh,* followed by a score of other scintillating productions; and as music-composer (alongside Louis Banks) for the Shakespearean ballet *Romeo and Juliet.* Is the hoary heritage of Kathak held untarnished, notwithstanding so many breath-taking changes?

Answers the ace Kathak danseuse Aditi Mangaldas, whose disciples put up trail-blazing performances on two successive evenings. “The only thing permanent in Kathak is change itself! Any art will go stale if there is no growth and no surge of constant creativity. Only changes that are enforced are bound to disappear, but the spontaneous changes are likely to remain there. In moving from the temple to the court, the ambience changed and story-telling needs disappeared. A form must adjust to its viewers who are watching and for whom it must carry meaning." Elaborating on what is forced, "I personally view *jugalbandis* between disparate forms as futile trends that don't flow into the next step and, therefore, unlikely to last."

The Kathak recitals by Gowri Diwakar and Rashmi Uppal, both advanced diploma-holders from 'Kathak Kendra', before coming under Aditi's tutelage, were pointers to the changes. Rashmi's overture: *Om Namah Shivaeh:* was clearly marked with very precise lines and *Natyadharmi* (stylised) in nature, in keeping with the accented rhymes of Adi Shankara's poetry. Gowri's traditional Kathak, in *Vasant Taal* (9-beat) – joined in frequently by Rashmi — comprised *Thaats, Tihais* and *Padhants,* bringing out how seamless flow and agility in speed could strengthen presentational beauty. Gowri's rendering of *Nikasi Chandni* in *Raga Megh Malhar* was a sensuous dance *in Shringara* mode. Dressed in sparkling white, she stressed romantic feelings with two *Gats* (short lyrics), often comparing the cool moonlight's attributes to earrings, pendants and bangles! *Shaam bhaye, Shyam nahin aye more dwaar...,* the finale in *Raga Madhumanti,* was an exquisitely composed piece on listless waiting in myriad patterns, — an exercise in poignancy.

Gowri avers about changes in Kathak, "They are fine, as long as there is no compromise in the basics. The main change is in the thought process, which has gone through 'contemporisation'. Viewers need new items, not repetition of the same traditional ones, and – as thinking beings – we've to keep that in mind all the time." Adds Rashmi, "Changes in Kathak in the past half-decade have been phenomenal, with costumes, stage-presence, music all undergoing radical changes, and themes reaching beyond the staple of Radha-Krishna. We dancers are educated today and have substantial media exposure. As long as one keeps to one's traditional roots, one should be welcome to make the thought-process contemporary. Spectators are well-read and have a lot of expectations."

Samve, was the "confluence of the five elements of nature that coalesce in complete harmony." Presented by Aditi under Drishtikon Dance Foundation, it aimed at the elements coming together harmoniously, awakening our sense of perfect equilibrium and invoking within our hearts and minds lasting bliss. *Earth* cited the *Atharva Veda: Pleasant be thy hills, O Earth, / Thy snow-clad mountains and thy woods! / Earth-brown, black, ruddy and multi-coloured. / On this Earth I stand, unvanquished, unslain, unhurt*... The dance by Anindita and Dheerendra was somewhat conventional. The tempo picked up with *Water* and its many nuances of flow, danced by the Gowri-Rashmi duo to Rachana's evocative verse: ...*Waterfalls, springs, sprightly streams and languid rivers, / You fill me with all your moods. / The vast seas, overpowering oceans merging into the horizon — / Wash me away, fill me with passion, romance and joy. / Your depth knows no limits, nor does my heart....*

The best was yet to come: with Rachana and other girls creating the most ineffable images of *Wind,* using *Darbari Kanada Sargams* sans any melody. Faiz Ahmad Faiz's ghazal came through resonantly: *Invisible / Intangible / Blowing softly or with vigour... / Bringing in messages of loved ones / Caressing me with passion and a painful gentleness / Engulfing me / And suddenly all the flowers, trees, gardens / Come alive with colours, fragrances, longings* ...From *Veda Sadhanam,* compiled by Sudhananda Bharati, came *Fire: You are effulgent, supreme Fire! Grant me spiritual effulgence, / You are the dynamic energy, grant me force. / You are strength, grant me physical, vital, mental and moral strength, / You punish the sinners, give me freedom from sins and evils....* The entire repertory visualised *Fire* through an enchanting *Tarana* in *Raga Yaman,* — a Samimulla Khan composition. *Space* was the grand finale in Ashutosh Dixit's poetry: *You sense me not, you see me not, / You touch me not, you hear me not, / Subtler than all you can feel, / Larger than your imagination steals, / But my essence and my seed / Forever will be my mystery*...The *sotto voce* mnemonics with the dancing quartet were unforgettable.

The last words are Aditi's, "Kathak's changing future belongs to both experiments and tradition. Experiments would explore new boundaries, grounded and strongly enriched by traditional inputs, to see what ultimate limits the dance can achieve. Everything said and done, there is only good dance and bad dance, that can easily demarcate what has been truly absorbed, practised and assimilated.!"

LOVE'S DIALOGUE WITH KATHAK: *Madhura Phatak*

It was a rare audio-visual treat. The petite Kathak danseuse Madhura Phatak sat on the stage and invoked Mira's lord with a lilting singing voice in *Raga Yaman*: *Maro Pranam, Banke Behari*.... She is seamlessly transformed into her dancing persona with a poetic text on her lips as a *Kathakar*: in the original incarnation of *Katha Vachan* (story-telling) of her dance-form. It is now Radha who, in her water-carrying palaver from the Yamuna, hears for the first time a distant flute: almost cajoling her to end its long wait. She is mesmerised and launches an eager search for the flute-player from Vrindavan's alley to alley, — in a coaxing lyric in the same *Yaman*: *Ajo Na Ayo Sajna Mera*.... The search has been long, with both fulfillments and frustrations, till it mingles with Mira's arduous quest in the confining chambers of Mewar, contrary to social canons

Madhura Phatak

of decorum and to the violation of conjugal norms. *Discovering Love: A Theatrical Dance Performance* is Madhura's choreographic and narrative oeuvre: connecting Radha and Mira over the aeons, — superbly supported by her elder sister Anuradha Sohoni in music. Radha, interestingly, does not occur in the epic *Mahabharata* or in Krishna's life-story *Srimat Bhagavata* or *Harivamsh.* Basically a *Puranic* character, she is given her due with Krishna in Jayadeva's *Gita Govinda* in the 12th century and only from Sri Chaitanya's time onwards, the endearing icons of Radha-Krishna duo is worshipped, with the Telugu saint-poet Nimbarka conferring godhood on Radha in Vrindavan. In sharp contrast, Mira is a real-life entity, whose childhood proclivity towards 'Girdhari Lal', disastrous marriage to the reigning Rana, eventual rejection of royal home and the roaming round, while singing her devout Bhajans are all historically vouched for.

In linking the two characters, Madhura has her own explanation, "Krishna has been an object of love in the Vaishnavite saint-poetry in India. To me, as a woman, there are two figures that strongly represent the human journey of love: Radha and Mira. Radha's love is for Krishna: in physical presence. Mira discovers the joy of loving the formless one. If Radha's love is wordless, full of non-verbal actions, Mira is very articulate about her love. A Radha finally matures into a Mira: by discovering that her Krishna lies within."

In the performance, Madhura goes farther and weaves – together with two disciples – her personal story as to how a girl has an inhibited upbringing in every way and still she has to look beautiful to be acceptable to others. She and Anuradha sing in English: *A Man is the sole path for a girl to her Womanhood...* How does this feminine assertion blend with the emotional surrender of both Radha and Mira to their lord? Madhura's spirited reply is, "This is how I've felt in my life and projected the feeling in my choreographed narrative. Krishna for me is a journey of re-connecting my own soul with that of the universe."

RAINDROPS ON DANCING BODIES:
Sharmistha Mukherjee

Kalidasa and Tagore, separated probably by a whole millennium, have one common thread: their infinite care for nature. All six seasons

Sharmistha Mukherjee's Group

of India are duly celebrated in their oeuvre, but while Kalidasa composed 28 poems each: as ode to rains and spring, Tagore devoted 114 songs to rains as opposed to 96 to spring: just short of a hundred. There is another distinction between the two literary giants. While Kalidasa's outpourings on rains are entirely physical and sensually eulogising: streaming clouds, hurtling thunderbolts, strutting peacocks, swollen rivers, charming woodlands, blue lotuses and fragrant flowers, beside bevies of beauteous, full-bodied women with cascading coiffure, — Tagore's rains gently eavesdrop into a myriad human emotions: where outside Nature and human nature invariably and imperceptibly intertwine with each other.

In her presentation of *Varsha Mangal* for ICCR's *Malhar Festival,* it was mainly a display of vintage Kathak: based on Tagore's evocation of rains. Says the petite choreographer Sharmistha Mukherjee, "I've confined myself to two emotions: *Milan* (union) and *Viraha* (separation). My selection of only nine songs falls squarely into these two genres, since they go hand-in-hand with Kathak. I've left out Tagore's lilting *Baul* compositions, which don't gel with my classical background. I've resorted to group choreography where vigorous aspects are highlighted and come down to solo for the mellowed moods experienced in solitude. There are many unknown emotions, too, whose stirrings leave one listless and I discarded rhythms there, too, since Kathak cadences cannot touch or caress them, where silence predominates over yearnings or deep pathos."

Scintillating footsteps are in sync for the overture: *Come, O my dark handsome one and fetch your nectar of companionship that rids one of all heat and thirst...* But the song, rendered in staccato style, is hardly authentic. This is the trouble throughout, — with the breakneck tempo ordained for the virility of pirouettes and dazzling footwork often runs counter to the spirit of *Laya* pervading in the original lyrics. In contrast, the song: *My desperation reverberates in the drums and the storm gathers afar in a dreadful silence...,* from the dance-drama *Shyama,* is well etched out. The all-time favourite: *Who are you, drawing the veil to hide your countenance and standing alone in my courtyard... is* possibly the best of the lot where Sharmistha discards her quicksilver rhythms and is the very picture of stillness. This is also true for: *My dear friend, I feel so restless in the darkened room, where my endless yearning cannot chart out its own path...*

The other songs, which seemed like verbal gymnastics, came and went, for instance, *The celestial drum echoes in my heart and shudders at the knitted eyebrows of the deep-set clouds...;* very Kathakesque peacock-posturing to: *My heart dances like a peacock with a rippling cadenza...; My thoughts are wafting with unseen winds, vibrant with an unreasonable sense of joy...; The Shravana skies are laden with gathering thunderstorms and it is the darkest of nights, how will you tread the mangrove-walk, O hapless lass?...* and the finale: *The cherished union is now on in the Shravana firmament, filled by the fragrance of Malati blossoms...*"Please realise that my Kathak dancers are not Bengali-speaking and it has been an uphill task to convey to them Tagore's poetic nuances," defends the choreographer. They did their valiant best, under the circumstances.

SOUNDS FROM SEVEN FORTS: *Parwati Dutta*

The neon-lit ramparts of the Old Fort, with every niche and cornice illumined tastefully, provided a wonderful backdrop to the Aurangabad-based troupe of Parwati Dutta. Hers was a recapitulation of some of the finest melodies and rhythms created by the practitioners of yore around the fortresses and citadels that their kings and Nawabs occupied and had their crunchy walls reverberate with the resonance of the sweetest songs and dances. What a lovely idea!

Srijan Tirth begins with a leisurely Dhrupad composition by Tansen in which he addresses Emperor Akbar in Agra Fort. Set in *Raga Mian Ki Malhar,* the master's own creation: *Shuva Muhurat,* the dancers' anklets resound into the corners of the sprawling space. The production flows into another panegyric: *Bhagya Vidhata, Tum Hi Ho Sukhadata*.... It is a *Bandish* and *Khayalnuma,* set to *Raga Devgiri Bilawal* created by Gopal Nayak at Devgiri Fort, Aurangabad, "We held our first musical concert there," declares the danseuse.

It is now a sonorous rendition of Pakhawaj and its intricate *Padhants* — sans any melody, but with a reverberating *Shiva Stotra,* the favourite of all Pakhawaj-players — that comes through with the group's finely-etched hand-gestures and footwork. The compositions are the handiwork of Raja Chhatrapati Singh at Bijnar Fort. An exquisite *Padam* follows, which was created decades ago by the king Swati Thirunal, seated in Tanjore Fort, — emphasising the *Alap Ang. Bandish* by Raja Chakradhar Singh of Raigarh Fort is the fifth fort highlighted.

Pandit Bindadin Maharaj, ancestor of Birju Maharaj's family, takes the viewers north now with a perennially favourite *Ashtapadi:*

Srijan Tirth

Bahe Pawana Sukhada Shital... created in his Awadh habitat. The concluding serenade is another Dhrupad by Tansen set to *raga Gurjari Todi.* Says Parwati, "Some musicologists aver that this special melody was dedicated to Empress Mriganayani of Gwalior Fort, who was herself a great artist." Does one savour the faint aroma of a romance there?

Adds Parwati, "Mine is a dancer's journey that re-discovers the glorious times of royal patronage to art. Spanning a period of a few hundred years, we cull out references to many traditions: created or sustained in this interregnum in the field of dance, music, percussion and literature. Our sojourn weaves together creations of three great artists and three great artist-monarchs. Our dance-delineation sequences the ethos of that by-gone era through the vision of each artist."

The finale was *Varna Riti,* chants of mnemonic syllables. The *Padhant* of the abstract language of the *Tala* system was treated as equivalent to the utterance of holy chants: *Jaya Govinda Jaya Gopala:* and danced with ecstasy, making it the best treat of the evening. Explains the director, "the syllables are not numerical arrangement of mnemonics on a time-scale, but find a deep connection to the sacred chants of our traditions. We've attempted to make our rhythmic *Padhants* — on the Pakhawaj – transcend the cerebral, seeking the spiritual."

Kathak Cameos from Kolkata: *Padatik*

Kathak is long held to be the art born out of the aural story-telling tradition flourishing in the Indo-Gangetic plane and its nerve-centres are traced to Lucknow, Jaipur and Banaras, each of which produced a dialect of the dance that had its own unique flavour. Of late, Raipur and partially North Bihar (thanks to Shovana Narain's research) have been added to this venerable list, but Kolkata and its contiguous region do not figure for Kathak anywhere.

Chetna Jalan, whose 'Padatik' group recently showcased some luminous Kathak, rubbishes that notion, "Kathak's roots can also be traced to the Purulia region of Bengal whose *Nachni* community performed nothing but Kathak, as evidenced in Company paintings preserved in Kolkata's Victoria Memorial. Those *Nachnis* – seen as forming forerunners of the marching British battalions – still exist in penny-packets there. The *Baijis* followed later in Kolkata and their *kothas* (dens) thronged in the Bowbazar area, to which I've been for learning purposes during childhood. Alaknanda Devi, sister of Sitara Devi, was a renowned *Baiji,* as also a teacher."

Adds She," The redoubtable Shambhu Maharaj established himself in Kolkata with dance-partner Vandana Sen and Ram Gopal-ji came from Jaipur with his sister Jai Kumari, who used to be our examiner in my mother's noted institution 'Sangeet Shyamala'. Ram Narain Mishra was another Kathak master, who taught Chitresh Das, just as Shambhu-*ji* trained Bela Arnab, both from the following generation. All senior dancers, indeed, learnt from those veterans and Kathak reigned supreme in Kolkata for long. Only afterwards came other gurus to us, like Kelucharan Mohapatra for Odissi, Maruthappa Pillai for Bharatanatyam, Bipin Singh for Manipuri and young Birju Maharaj for Kathak."

Vividha, the Padatik presentation, opened with *Abahan,* a brilliant invocation from *Prithvi Sutra* of Rig *Veda* with music – based mainly on sarod and Kathak mnemonics — conceptualised by Pt. Jasraj. The talented duo, Ritushree and Suman, wove a filigree of *Lasya* and *Tandava* movements: using liberally balletic hugs, aerial lifts and caressing of mother earth. Avers Ritushree, who thought of the idea, "We explored vibrancy in inner space; within a human being and in outer space: informing external nature. Then we reached out for *Vyom* (the void). It was re-discovering ourselves in relation to earth..."

Srishti, the grand finale with all nine dancers, was an arresting piece for its music as well as choreography. Explains Chetna, "Music was created by Birju Maharaj with Louis Banks, visiting repeatedly the latter's Mumbai studio. This was organised some ten years back, before their collaborative work for *Romeo & Juliet* was thought of. Back in Kolkata, Maharaj-*ji* superimposed *bols* (mnemonics) in multiple layers. Choreography visualised the primordial act of creation: with twinkling stars and streaking meteors, captured through well-orchestrated body-movements and confirmed by sparkling, figure-hugging, light-hued costumes, — rather than colourful frilly clothes of conventional Kathak. Incidentally, I strongly feel that both dress and demonstrations of traditional Kathak are now insipid and quoting constantly the heritage of forefathers is devoid of any meaning, if you're not creating legacy for your own successor generations!" Any takers?

JINGLING ANKLETS IN SPRING:
Saswati Sen, Malti Shyam

Pt. Birju Maharaj has reached the biblical age-span of 'three scores and ten' and it is good news that he is wonderfully alive still taking his ordained art forward. Among countless touching tributes to their guru is one from the senior most disciple Saswati Sen, "My mentor, guide, friend, ideal, — may he live an eternal life to guide us towards true art," and another, "He has taught us to love dance. He has taught us that rhythm is everywhere. He is the reason why many of us dance." 'Kalashram', his dream institute founded after he ended his tenure with 'Kathak Kendra', is also moving from glory to glory, the latest evidence of which is *Vasantotsava,*. Meanwhile there have been 12 major dance-dramas and ballets (including the phenomenal success *Romeo and Juliet*), and some thirteen short productions in a period of less than eight years since Kalashram's inception.

Was spring given prominence by the dancers? Explains Saswati, the prime mover of the 3-day festival, "Artistes kept that in mind, but no theme as such was laid out. Celebrating Maharaj-*ji's* turning

70, we responded to his wish to emphasis only pristine purity of technical Kathak where there would be no copying from one another or choreographic extravaganza. His ethos is that there should first be a firm grounding and then the flowering of talent could follow. In this special year, we've mapped out a programme for every month – covering Delhi, NOIDA, Jamshedpur and Kolkata – with programmes like *Pratibha Festival* for upcoming talents; *Krishna – the Eternal* in music, dance and poetry; and *Sadhana Festival* presenting young talents; besides seminars and workshops."

Also remembering Jeevan Pani and Keshav Kothari, whom Delhi's art world has lost recently, says Saswati, "Jeevan-*da* pointed out how an institute exists for the dancers and not vice versa. And Keshav-*ji* taught us the importance of good organisation and the importance of even an aesthetic invitation-card." Adds Maharaj-*ji,* "Keshav was my student-mate in our learning days, occupied the same room and shared such luxury-food as homemade soup and bread for daily dinner! He egged me on to go further, as did my later dance-partner

Saswati Sen

Kumudini Lakhia. They are very largely responsible for what I'm today,"

The festival opened with scintillating displays of pure dance – by both young and senior performers – mostly in the popular *Teentaal.* After felicitation of the tabla maestro Pt. Kishan Maharaj, the brother-duo Prabhakar and Divakar Mishra followed with Hindustani vocal. Meticulously trained by Pts. Rajan and Sajan Mishra, they rendered *Raga Jog* in *Vilambit Alap* and a *Drut* composition. Later, young Prashant Shah, the ace disciple of Kumudini Lakhia, put up an impressive *Jugalbandi* with Rajasthani Langa and Mangniyar singers who came front-stage to accompany the dancer with lilting songs and matching *Khadtals.* After Sandip Mallick brought a touch of Kolkata and Sandeed Mahavir showed presentational flourish of the West where he directs 'AMS Compan', came Rajendra Gangsani, the torch-bearer of Jaipur, and brought the house down by inviting Maharaj-*ji* to accompany him impromptu on tabla. Describes Saswati, "Tabla literally sings in Maharaj-*ji's* hands and, with Fateh Singh on Pakhawaj, it was a veritable *Trigalbadi* (threesome)!"

Next evening, Malti Shyam provided the first touch of spring by dancing to a Thumri: *Holi Aure Rangi Bhari Bhayo*.... Her languorous movements and soft leaps were captivating. Following on tabla, the teenager Shubh Maharaj, grandson of Kishan Maharaj, regaled with *Uthan* and *Gats* of his family-vintage at various beats like 5, 2/3 and 4. Among senior danseuses, Kajal Sharma showed technical prowess in 14 and 16 beats, Prerana Shrimali followed with an unusual Shiva-*stuti: Rangeela Shambhu Gora Le Padhay*... and Durga Arya with traditional guru-*stuti* and *Teentaal* in *Vilambit* and *Madhya Layas.* But what culminated the evening was a special presentation of Maharaj-*ji's Abhinaya* to Kishen Maharajs poetry. It was a gala *Pas de Deux.* Concludes Saswati, "We discovered by sheer chance that Kishen Maharaj-*ji* wrote poetry and thereafter to persuade our guru to do *Bhao Batana* became an easy task!"

FROM SCHUBERT TO KATHAK: *Shovana Narayan, Athreyee Roy, Shreya Sharan, and Madhura Phatak*

The Austrian Embassy pulled a minor scoop by presenting a selection of four musical pieces by the Austrian composer Franz Peter Schubert in the Kathak dance-form, to a discerning audience. “This is real fusion between Indian classical dance and Western classical music,” responds an enthusiastic Himachal Som, former director general of ICCR. “Perhaps pure Kathak or Bharatanatyam items have become blasé, with countless performances behind them!”

Schubert (1797-1828) is justly famous in the music world for his Trout piano quintet (1819), C major symphony (1825) and B minor symphony (1822), known as Unfinished. But he is particularly

Schubert: Shovana Narayan & Disciples

remembered as the greatest exponent of German songs (*Lieders*), which number around 600. "There is a lot of commonality between Schubert's Lieders and our songs," muses Shovana Narayan who choreographed the pieces. "In both genres, a wide range of moods occur and emotions are all-encompassing. As a result, there is a lot of scope of *Abhinaya* at an interpretational level that depicts love or loneliness: particularly with *Bhav Batana* of our idiom. We can also work in various realms: direct narrative, subtly suggestive, or even highly philosophical."

The first *Lieder* was *The Beloved Colour: I will dress in green./ In green weeping willows / My love is so fond of green / I will seek a cypress grove* …. Athreyee Roy and Shreya Sharan donned verdure green odhnis and configured an abstract dance, in tune with soft German music. The second piece was *Loneliness,* danced by Shovana: *Like a mournful cloud / Passing through the clear air / —- So I wend my way / Onward with halting step / Through bright happy life lonely and ungreeted*…She was in turn serious and morose, and mirrored a hapless individual passing through the journey of life. The third *Lieder* was *Rain of Tears*, a poignant piece, for which Madhura Phatak enacted a man, alternately in a sad and happy mood: *In the company of his ladylove, I saw her nod and glance up / from the happy brook / the little blue flowers on the bank / Nodded and glanced back at her / and the whole sky seemed sunk in the brook*...

All these pieces needed copious emoting and *Bhav* had to flow out, — which was not always the case. The need for a taut orchestration of glances, gestures and movements was sorely felt, although the sensitivity of the lines came through. The last poem was *Erl King* by the great German poet Johann Wolfgang von Goethe. Here was the legend of Death fleeting through the forest and trying to snatch the distraught youth: all the time unseen by the youth's anxious father. It opened as: *Who is riding so late through the night and wind? / It is the father with his child / —- "My son, why do you hide your face so fearfully?" / "Father, can you not see the Erl King? / The Erl King with crown and train?" / "My son, it is a streak of mist*"—- Madhura as father and Athreyee as son made an impressive duo, but Shovana was at her imperial best as Erl King with a majestic robe.

The closing was*: The father shudders, he rides fast / He holds the groaning child in his arms / Arrives home in toil and travail / In his arms the child was dead*... Goethe's *Lieder* evoked the best of Kathak from the dancing trio: father, son and Death: with all the dazzling virility and vivacity, grace and grandeur, that belong to the Kathak idiom.

FROM FREEZES TO FLUIDITY: *Nadim Siddiqui*

It was an extraordinary phenomenon. On a bare stage swathed by translucent light-rays, the dancer stood motionless, – with her back to the viewers and with outstretched arms, ostensibly absorbed in prayer. Slowly the fingers trembled, the arms twirled and the torso turned halfway, revealing a face with half-closed eyes lost in meditation. The body then turned around and lurched forward in a quicksilver motion. The dancer traversed the stage: with gestures and movements that were steeped in spirituality....

Nadim Siddiqui, the celebrity Kathak danseuse from Pakistan, was that rare breed of artists whose every inflexion spoke volumes, each gesture was suffused with the other-worldly meaning. Says Nadim, "When I dance, I am on a 'high' and the material surrounding me becomes nil. It is a needle-front focus that annihilates the ego. For, if ego lingers, you cannot shoot down senses." Is it a totally Sufi mindset? Smiles the dancer, "It's *Masti* for me always that's not deliberate but overwhelms my entire person when I perform. It's Bulle Shah's *Tere ishq nachayaa...*"

The highly-subdued recital began in *Raga Jayjawanti: Vinki ko kahiye re baahi...,* a Bade Ghulam Ali composition as an *Abhinaya* piece. The second one was another Khan-Sa'ab composition in *Raga Kedar: Naveli naar ban-tan nikli...* with plenty of *Sargam* and *Taankari,* to catch with the mood of plentiful decorative adornments, and with percussion-support from Pakistan's veteran *Pakhawaj-nawaz* Allah Lok. The third composition – yet another vintage Bade Ghulam —- was in *Raga Rageshwari: Shuv din aye...* with frenzied ecstasy and stilled serenity punctuating each other. The finale was Nadim's own pure dance of *Lehra* – punching freezes with fast tempo — to the melody of *Raga Jayjajawanti* again.

How does she carry so effortlessly the essence of Sufism in every movement of hers? Beams Nadim, "Sufiana has a *Ru* (face) that is suffused with Allah's *Nur* (light)! My whole physique becomes a beacon-light for Khudah, who's my one and only *Piya* (beloved). In the UK, I was immersed in Sufiana for 16-17 productions of mine and put into my Kathak a lot of Sufism. My great favourites are Maulana Rumi, Hazrat Amir Khusrau and Baba Bulle Shah." On how such long stretches materialised in the UK, she reminisces, "I was banished from Pakistan in Zia-ul's time in 1979 and could return only in 1984 for short spells. You see, people in Pakistan give me a lot of respect, but there isn't much public viewing of dance due to security risk. Private shows are OK". Questioned about any major production in the UK, she surprises one by her reply, "My most recent work is a one-hour ballet, *Krishna,* under the aegis of Royal Ballet. Krishna is played by a Swede, Kit; Radha is Litisha from France; and the Gopis are 30 highly-trained ballerinas from the Royal Ballet. It's a large-scale performance where I've mixed Kathak with modern ballet (especially for its leaps) and used a stage that's almost a reality-show. How I wish I could bring the production to India, — where I want to come back again and again for resuscitation!"

Reverting back to her upbringing, recalls Nadim, “My first training was in Lahore for 10-12 years, from Ghulam Hussain. He was affectionately called ‘Maharaj’, being an ardent disciple of the great Achchan Maharaj. Not being himself a performer, he sent me to the latter’s son Birju Maharaj to hone my skills. I’ve been learning from this legendary guru since 1980 and I’ll never cease to learn. My Kathak cannot go beyond what he has taught me and this evening I’ve been singularly lucky to dance in his presence.” To such a deep sense of obeisance, Maharaj-*ji's* subsequent response is equally touching, “Nadim had come to me from Hussain as a grown-up person, but what she imbibed from me and what she demonstrated today has three sterling qualities: *Itminaan* (composure), *Pyaar* (love) and *Tasalli* (authenticity).” What a beautiful reciprocation between the teacher and the student! When conveyed this feedback from guru, Nadim bursts into tears and there are no words anymore…

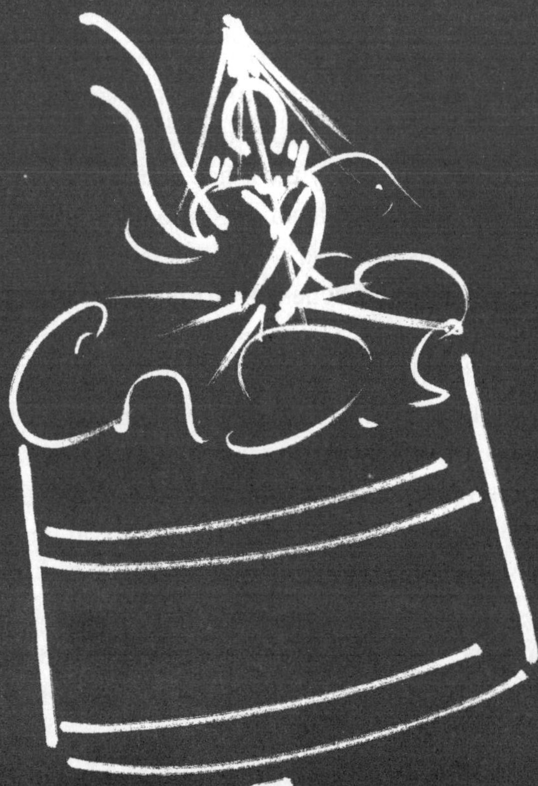

Manipuri

R.K. Singhajit Singh

Overview

by R.K. Singhajit Singh

Contemporary situation of Manipuri Dance needs to be viewed from different angles as the style belongs to an era of untouched purity as well as the demands of a wider horizon. The dance and music of Manipur are so different from the other art forms of India that a common point of reference is usually found inadequate to understand and appreciate them.

Born in the temples and still inextricably woven into the fabric of the people's religious life, it is difficult to view the Manipuri performing arts in isolation from its natural matrix. The style and its aesthetics are influenced by the ethos and sensibilities of a living culture. Even the advent of Vaishnavism took on a native appearance, enriching the religious sentiment with a new identity and also making Manipuri dance one of the richest art forms thriving in the very life and breath of a people. The *Mandapa* tradition of *Sankirtana* is becoming stronger by the day, as it is an indispensable part of Manipuri religious life. *Raas Lila* presentations, however, have suffered because of various reasons including high cost of production, time-consuming rehearsals involving school-going children and the present-day political situation in the state where night performances are not always possible.

When the art was transplanted from *Mandapa* to the proscenium stage, the need for a new orientation became obvious. What is good for the temple is not necessarily good for the stage. The journey from the religious surrounding to the secular ambience led to various developments and natural adaptations. A new attitude of professionalism has emerged where child Krishna and Radha, so much adored in the *Mandapa* for their innocence, could not meet the demanding standards of professional dancing. Now, therefore, Radha and Krishna played by grown-up girls have become the accepted norm for the stage. Interestingly, a girl playing Krishna has been found more acceptable than a boy. This is only one example. While still performing excerpts culled out from the *Mandapa Lilas* on the stage, many talented dancers and choreographers have ventured out of the traditional themes, producing some excellent works. They have enhanced the vocabulary of movements and enriched the presentations. The connoisseurs of Manipur welcome these new works and the emerging innovations as long as the purity of the style is maintained, but any deviation distorting the character of the dance is rejected.

Although solo dance pieces were there in the *Raas*, they were always intrinsic to the *Lilas*. Solo dances specifically designed for the stage is a fresh and welcome development and some artistes have done exceedingly well in this regard. The tremendous variety and versatility of Manipuri, ranging from the softest to the most vigorous, has proved to be a boon for choreographers both in dance-dramas and solos, and many such works have won wide appreciation.

The more vigorous aspects of Manipuri Dances with drums like the *Pung Cholom* and *Dhol Cholom* and *Thang-Ta* (martial arts) are in great demand all over the world because of their great vigour, speed, turns and spins. These natural crowd-pooling qualities are typical of the popular taste of our times. Like every kind of classical art, Manipuri is also evolving all the time while maintaining the typical characteristics of being soft, lyrical and subdued. The present period is most important for the Manipuri artists, as they are struggling to express their identity in different directions.

Any art thrives with the effective communication between the performer and the audience. While the artistes are doing their best to preserve and project Manipuri at its best, the art-lovers also have an aesthetic responsibility to transcend their own cultural conditioning to accept meaningfully what could be alien to their natural sensibilities and savour the extremely rich flavors of the art. Indeed, it is one of the purest and richest art forms, which deserves fullest adulation from the discerning audience.

THE WAGER ON A WOMAN: *Priti Patel*

The dimly-lit evening sees the vast fountain lawns transformed into a gigantic chequered-board. On the sprawling black-and-white squares are the dancers moving around in fascinating formations: in intertwining curves, diagonals and long arcs. While the seven girls traipse on rhythmic steps, the half-a-dozen boys have the virile horse-like agility, — often moving out of the arena and crouching, to leap upon the platform. It becomes clear soon that they are the pawns of a game, — dispersed and re-assembled in multiple groups. *The Throw of Dice,* the choreographic extravaganza, begins with the master-players seen frozen on the upper thrones, somberly contemplating the moves and often silently gesticulating their ecstasy or exasperation.

Says Priti Patel, the petite director from Kolkata, "My work is inspired by the *Mahabharata* theme of games between the Pandavas and Kauravas, which portrays deceit and greed: the cause of the Great War. In Manipuri language, *Sanaba* means playing games and we all are *Sanaroi:* players in these games. I use many of the indigenous ploys, with *Augri,* for instance, taken from *Lai Haraoba* dance of yore. *Panthali,* where boys surround the women and execute

Priti Patel's Group

threatening circles, is another one. In fact, I've been fond of games since own childhood, having learnt many from my uncle!"

The tempo mounts and now the white-bedecked woman appears in enticing *Lasya.* The narrator's 'my beautiful wife' does not refer to Draupadi by name, but it is the same agony, a woman's wailing appeal to the seniors and the anger at the ultimate ignominy of exposure in full public view. She symbolises all women and people fight among themselves over her red cloth. Help delayed is help denied and, in fiery moments of angst and disgust, husbands take pledge, having been defeated in an unfair game. The women's procession with burning torches epitomises the terror and its aftermath.

"When the queen is pawned in the game, it's nothing but an old legacy," contends Priti. "A Manipuri king, having 99 wives and concubines, is known in earlier days to fight battles with Burma and Tripura, and share their beautiful women as the booty! Tonu Leijing Lembi was one of the queens who was wagered upon in recorded history. The queens symbolised money and property. In our society, the powerful players still control every aspect of social and economic structure. It is their motif that counts above all!"

The Throw of Dice transcends its epic allusion and becomes symbolic of today's Manipur where there is a battle for body and mind. "The worst sufferers are innocent women and children," avers the director. "I've a personal message based on my life-experience and I refer to Manipur which is burning. Everyone is playing a game. It's in the nature of men: since the very primitive times!"

WHITE MESSENGER IN BLUE SKY: *Chaotombi Singh*

In Kalidasa's masterpiece *Meghadutam,* the imagery invests the landscape with a personality. When the love-lorn Yaksha, for instance, tells the cloud about the river Gambhira with her clear waters, 'a tranquil pool of consciousness,' and 'those dazzling upward leaps of glittering fishes bright as water lilies', which are her welcoming glances, — what he is seeing and narrating is not the landscape, but the long-separated beloved Yakshi. In Kalidasa's immortal poetry, landscapes are specific, yet symbolic, and the natural world and the human world both participate in the divine.

It is this divine aspect that informs the dance-drama *Meghdoot,* presented by Jawaharlal Nehru Manipur Dance Academy, Imphal. Choreographed by Sangeet-Natak awardee Chaotombi Singh, it does show Yaksha's thoughts, shaped by *Viraha* (separation), but the mindsets of all the characters are imbued with *Bhakti* (devotion). Says Chaotombi, "I've begun the play with a *Purbaranga* in the true Sanskrit dramatic tradition. Hence my use of elements of *Nata Sankirtana* in the overture, is steeped in devotion." It is a colourful foreplay: in the subdued Manipuri dance-idiom.

Departing from the poetic text, *Meghdoot* stages, in flashback, an elaborate worship of Shiva by the divine treasurer Kuvera where everybody is present, but not Yaksha who is immersed in his love-play with Yakshi. The enraged Kuvera separates the two and banishes Yaksha from Alakapuri, his abode. The meandering lover is highly distracted and lands in Ramagiri, pining for his ladylove. Notes Kalidasa: *The impassioned lover having passed some months... / saw on Asadha's most auspicious day / a cloud embracing the crest of the hill, / strikingly shaped like a sportive elephant / bent down to butt a riverbank....* Here a bevy of Manipuri maidens sway and swerve in *Bhangi Pareng* forming the blue clouds on the mountain-peaks. Yaksha entreats them to take his message to the far-away Alakapuri. The estranged Yaksha contemplates his past and prays for one single chance to have a lovers' union. Chaotombi avers, "I've shown in my choreography clouds carrying the message, getting away with his heartbeats as well." It comes through beautifully in the compositions on stage.

Over hills and dales, forests and rivers, the messenger-clouds float away in their long sojourn to the high Himalayas. In the last phase, the flock of white swans from the lake Mansarovar joins them: in a balletic *tour de force.* The focus gets shifted to Yakshi: lost in reverie, with people prompting her to take the path of *Bhakti.* Yakshi is now draped in saffron clothes, —with *Sankirtana* going round. The finale is a grand union in Alakapuri again, with the lover duo joining Kuvera, and all is forgiven. In the highly *Natya Dharmi* dance and décor, the many departures from the classic poet are also forgiven!

Kathakali

Deepti Omcheri Bhalla

Overview

by Deepti Omcheri Bhalla

Kathakali, the classical theatre art form of Kerala, is the perfect example of total theatre—a harmonious blend of music, drama and gestures – that journeyed from temple theatre to modern stage. Over the years, it has grown popular not only for its grandeur but also its highly stylised technique and dramatic presentation.

Modem choreographers both Indian and foreign living outside Kerala, recognising the unique techniques, have incorporated many of its elements in their contemporary choreographic presentations, which eventually became their masterpieces, winning them accolades world over. The great poet Rabindranath Tagore, having seen the spectacular drama which had the rare other-worldly charm, introduced it in Santiniketan at its centre of arts that he founded, about eight decades ago.

This magnificent art form evolved from simpler devotional forms like 'Krishnattam' and 'Ramanattam', which did not have elaborate acting conventions. A few characters in these theatre presentations wore masks and the actors themselves sang their dialogues in verses. Kathakali, incorporating the graces of these forms, discarded masks, discontinued the oral expressions, and expanded itself to emerge as a highly intricate and stylised-theatre art form of Kerala.

History says that King Manaveda relieved the actors from singing by introducing vocalists to sing Kathakali songs from behind so that the actors could render their visual interpretation through gestures. It was Vettath Naatu Raja who introduced 'Chenda' as an important percussion instrument; he also replaced the masks with 'Cutti', the make up. Kottayam Tampuran made the technique more intricate and stylised. Veteran actors — with their own genius and creative ability — further intensified and broadened the art. All these led to the evolution of an uncommon theatrical art form, which communicated worldly virtues and values through unworldly characters and themes.

Till the seventies, the attraction mainly was on its colourful costume and make-up that built a supernatural aura around it. Kathakali became an indispensable part of Indian tourism promotion. Their presentations were less understood but more admired for an ambience of grandeur that it created. Attempts to popularise Kathakali by introducing modern themes with non-Puranic and contemporary themes and characters had started from the days of poet Vallathol who was responsible for the regeneration of the art. Plays based on the life of Gandhi, and stories of David and Goliath, Mary Magdalene, Rustom and Sohrab were written and presented with all seriousness, yet they all failed to create any sustained impact. They were not appreciated by the purists who felt those themes and characters would not go into the mould of Kathakali, which gave scope for building the unique theatrical experiments through an aura of supernatural and unrealistic beings.

The seventies saw many cultural contacts and exchanges between India and abroad when scholars and artistes from overseas realised the great potential that lay in the technique of Kathakali, which somehow got subdued and overlooked because of the language and elaborate presentational practices. More and more foreigners came and lived in Kerala to learn and understand this great art in its pristine form. This heralded a period of creative interest in Kathakali among the theatre lovers all over the world, and traditional and modern plays abroad. More than its spectacular visual appeal, the intricate and stylised dramatic elements in the art, and the real essence of Kathakali got amazing appreciation.

More experimentation followed with adaptation of Shakespearean plays, Greek classics and French classical works, — all excelling through the medium of Kathakali. The texts were scripted and edited to suit the style. The language remained *Manipravalam,* a combination of Sanskrit and Malayalam. While retaining the traditional make-up and costume, modifications were made to suit the new characters and their cultural milieu. Even the orchestra included a few more instruments, selected from the traditional lore — like *Kombu* (a long curved wind instrument), *Timila* (a drum) and flute for creating better situational impact. As different from the earlier scripts which had long texts that suited more the elaborate conventional acting, the experimental plays were brief and gave more scope for interpolations — bridging the gap between the actor and the non-traditional audience.

The Kathakali music rendered in *Sopana* style (traditional music dramatically rendered), which adopted only those conventional *Ragas* or melodies that suited for creating dramatic impact, has now included melodies from Indian classical music both Karnatak and Hindustani for enhancing the melodic appeal.

Emerging from the orthodoxy of the temple precincts, Kathakali has spread its appeal and grandeur all over the world and yet retains its mystical elegance and distinctive nature. It flies high with its feet positioned well on the ground!

WHEN DIVINITY TOUCHES HUMANITY: *K Unnikrishnan*

Kathakali, the venerable classical dance-style of Kerala, really belongs to the world of theatre. The word literally means 'story-play', and can be called dance-drama, ballet, opera, pantomime or miracle-play – or all rolled into one – but never a solo dance like other classical forms. The International Centre for Kathakali, established in Delhi in 1960, has been rendering yeoman's service to promote this art, as was evident from their just-concluded Kathakali festival. Their Principal, Kalamandalam Unnikrishnan, elaborates –

Why is the international centre For Kathakali (ICK) located in the Capital rather than the state to which it belongs?

There're already a number of institutions in Kerala which are propagating the form, starting with Mahakavi Vallathol's 'Kerala Kalamandalam'. The others are 'PSV Natya Sangam', 'Gandhi Seva Sadan' and 'Margi'. ICK's the only one of its kind that is devoted to the broad spectrum of Kathakali and allied arts outside the state.

Are there other bodies that espouse the cause of this old form?

There are several Kathakali clubs in Kerala that work for this art. In Delhi, too, there is 'Todayam' who arranges regular Kathakali programmes, at least 2-3 in a year. Although the times have changed, it's mainly the Kerala temples that still hold dance-festivals, although there are demands to stage dance-dramas of other forms as well. Even films have taken up the cause, like *Vaanaprastham* that depicted the life of a dedicated dancer and proved immensely popular, helping the cause.

Talking of changed times, have any changes come in the traditional contents of Kathakali dance-dramas?

From the ICK, we've been trying out experimental themes, quite frequently in fact. We've done Greek plays like *Bachae* and taken them to Greece. Shakespeare's work has been attempted, like *King Lear, Macbeth* and *Othello,* of course in Malayalam. Traditional Christian stories like *Mary Magdalene* and *David & Goliath* and Buddhist parable like *Chandala Vikshuni* (by Tagore) have been enacted with success. Tagore's *Sacrifice, Chandalika* and *Chitrangada* were done as well as the Persian classic *Rustam-Sohrab.* We've done historical persons and events like *Bhakta Mira, Bhakti Deepika* (on Sankaracharya), *Jhansi Ki Rani* and *Bhava Suddhi,* the last one on Humayu's infatuation for someone's married queen and sparing her, when accosted as 'brother'! Kalidasa's *Kumara Samvabam* and *Meghadootam* were done by us. Even in the traditional epics and *Puranas,* less-known stories have been culled out, like *Purohit Ravana* (on Ravana acting as Rama's priest) and *Taranisena* (on Lakshmana's son). We've taken classics from our neighbourhood Tamil Nadu and done *Bhakta Nandanar* and *Kavi Kokilam...*

All of the above are in Malayalam, but how about other Indian languages?

We performed *Rashmi Rathi* (Sun's Charioteer), on Karna's life, based on the famous eponymous Hindi poem by Dinkar. But the Capital's audience didn't seem to take to it much.

Kathakali's staple seems to be its more-than-life-size characters. What are they?

Yes, they're symbolic types and fall into six distinct categories. *Pacha* (green) is for good, noble and romantic characters like Arjuna, Nala, etc., in green make-up; *Kathi* (knife) is for villains, and aggressive characters: with knife-like patterns around nose; *Thadi* (beard) is either red beard for evil and wicked ones, or white beard for Hanumana, or black beard for forest-dwellers and hunters; *Kari* (black) is for demons; *Minukku* (radiant) for characters of gentleness and high spiritual quality; and *Theppu* (with painting and special make-up) for birds and animals.

Are there changes coming over time in techniques and support system?

There's no great change, except that electric lights are often used to have certain areas lit up or create dark zones for achieving dramatic effects. Slight changes have crept in costumes, too, but all within the frame of traditional Kathakali. Music continues to be the *Sopanam* style of staccato kind, but, of late, Carnatic *ragas* have been introduced. Musical instruments continue to be the same, namely, *Chenda, Edekka, Mardalam* and large cymbals.

How about training and the rigour of pre-dawn oil-massages?

(Smiling)The rigour is still there, but the pre-dawn regimen has vanished! The full-time 8-year courses of Kalamandalam or ICK have all become part-time, as there are other demands on time for students these days, who have their own educational curriculum to pursue. But the enthusiasm continues unabated and, in fact, many younger teachers – apart from performers – have materialised in place of old gurus and the audience-response is definitely not on the wane!

A last question, — are you in favour of propagating Kathakali's powerful repertoire of gestures and movements, without the forbidding make-up of the traditional kind?

Yes, there's a need as well as demand for this. When we give demonstrations under SPIC-MACAY or visit Centre of Cultural resource & and Training (CCRT) centres in Delhi, Hyderabad or Udaipur, we do elaborate on our highly-developed body-language, sans the make-up!

Kathakali Guru: Sadanan Balakrishnan

SPARKLING GLORY OF KATHAKALI

Kathakali has been described by the cognoscente as the 'Art of the 'Non-worldly'. .Few performing art-forms are marked by the dramatic dynamics that govern Kathakali. The dance, stemming from the culturally-rich Kerala, is characrterised by its unique feature of maintaining distance from worldly reality and selects to include — within its scope – only the most supernatural and mythological aspects: concerning the lives and affairs of celestial beings, deities, demons and sages.

For almost half a century, the International Centre for Kathakali (ICK) has been maintaining a performing troupe of 20 artists (including 8 dancers, 2 Chenda / Edekka players, 2 Maddalam players, 3 vocalists and 2 make-up men, among others) who hold over 60 performances every year in India. Besides, they fly the flag of Kathakali in the USA, Canada, Latin Americas, Europe, South East Asia and Australia. Their participation has become a regular hallmark in the international arena through the Athens Festival; Asian Festival of Traditional Dance and Music, Tokyo; International Ramayana Festival, Cambodia;; Indian Ocean Festival, Perth; Asia-Pacific Festival, Wellington; Manizales Theatre Festival, Columbia; Cervantio Festival, Mexico; Early Music Festival, Holland; and Delphi Festival, Greece.

Says Kalamandalam Unnikrishnan, who heads ICK, "To maintain its fairly impressive record, ICK and its ten centres in Delhi enroll about 130 students (annually about 50) in different fields of Kathakali, such

Kathakali Play 'David & Goliath'

Kathakali Play 'Taranisena'

as, dance, vocal music, percussion instruments (Chenda, Maddalam and Edekka), *Chutty* (make-up) and costume They undergo both extensive and intensive courses, for which enthusiasm is not uniform and some students do leave in the midstream, thinking of their future. But senior students of our Kathakali School are also good artists!"

The dramatic quality is amply evident in the annual anniversary of the Kathakali School where a large crop of plays — written poetically in 'Manipravalam' language that is an admixture of Malayalam and Sanskrit – are enacted every year, relying mainly on traditional sources like the *Ramayana,* the *Mahabharata* and the *Bhagavata.* The recent anniversary festival, for instance, brought three interesting features to the fore. One, the number of girl-students was very large. "It's almost 80%," confirms the Principal. One wonders why, then, women do not figure in the Centre's permanent repertory. Two, the verse-plays are set to appropriate *Ragas* and it is the singer – accompanied by the drums and large cymbals – who literally controls the actual performance on stage. Three, the episodes often reveal many fascinating socio-cultural angles and these are illustrated below in a few of the epic episodes.

In *Subhadra Haranam,* there is a justifiable rage of Balabhadra, Krishna's brother, on hearing about Arjuna's treacherous abduction of their dear sister Subharda, but he calms down when Krishna tactfully points out that killing Arjuna would only leave Subhadra bereaved.

A calamity is similarly averted by wise counselling. In *Narakasura Vadham,* the demon Naraka's beautiful maid, Nakrathundi, is sent to abduct the heavenly maidens but she loses her heart by looking at the handsome prince Jayantha, son of Indra, and make amorous advances to the youth. The strong borderline between the divine and the demonic worlds is thus blurred, defying prevailing social norms. In *Lava-Kusha Samvad,* Lava and Kusha, playing in the forest, notice the sacrificial horse, sent around by Rama and capture the animal, when their adversary, Hanumana, discovers the two children's resemblance with Rama and is unable to offer a proper fight. What a heart-warming sight! In *Kiratam,* Arjuna – doing penance in the forest to Shiva for obtaining the weapon of *Pashupat* — fights fiercely against Shiva in disguise, over the ownership of a wild boar killed by both their arrows. When Arjuna is badly mauled in battle, he is kindly forgiven and bequeathed the mighty weapon, but not before he has learnt not to be arrogant again!

There aero many such charming anecdotes, essayed with gusto by the youthful Kathakali dancers, mostly vivacious girls! "Kathakali plays are written like Shakespeare's plays and are available in book form," informs Unnikrishnan. They are surely of lasting value!

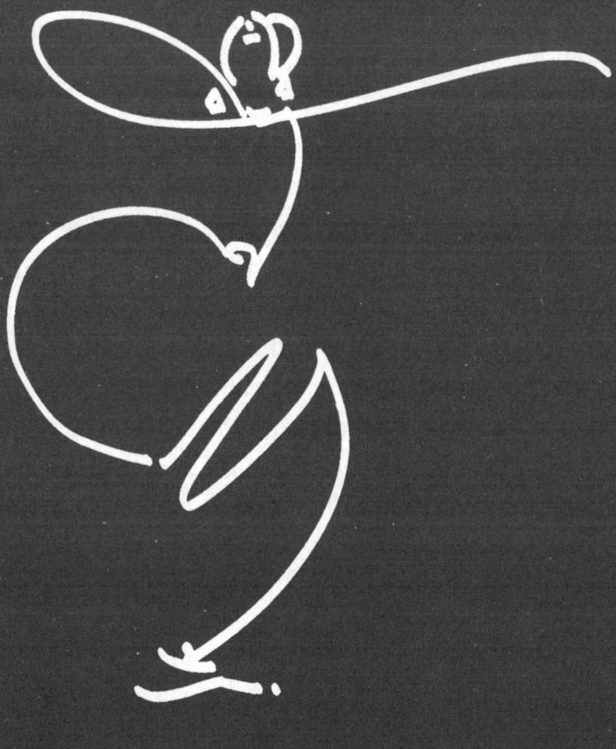

Mohiniyattam

Jayaprabha Menon

Overview

by Jayaprabha Menon

Mohiniyattam, the lyrical dance form of Kerala, is rich with *Lasya* movements. The gentle and graceful swaying of the torso and the circular movements known as *Chuzhippu* are the characteristics of Mohiniyattam. Mohiniyattam has gone through several phases of revival and has now evolved as a beautiful dance form with distinction from the other major classical dances of India. The introduction of *Sopana Sangeeta,* the regional music of Kerala and the regional temple instruments like the *Edakka* and *Maddalam* adds to the regional flavour of the art form.

Mohiniyattam has been embellished and nourished by incorporating more regional elements and concepts from other art forms like the *Naagyarkoothu*, *Thiruvathirakali*, *Patayani, Kalari,* etc. The usage of regional percussion instruments, mentioned above, highlights the nuances of the movements. Mohiniyattam is probably the only art form where every footfall is enhanced with a corresponding body movement. The percussion instruments and the rhythm cycle or the *Tala* pattern are entirely in keeping with the unique character that relates to the regional ethos. .The regional *Talas,* such as, the *Marma Tala* (14 beats), *Kumbha Tala* (20 beats), *Ayyadi* or *Panchar*i *Tala* (6 beats) — where there are counts in beats and silence — are unique and characteristically regional. These are used with *Vaitharis* (counts) in the repertoire of Mohiniyattam.

This beautiful as well as graceful art form now has a very rich and wide repertoire with a variety of traditional items likes the *Ashtapadis, Ayaanis, Niram Tathvam,* etc. More and more research and innovations are going on in the field of Mohiniyattam. The future of Mohiniyattam is safe in the hands of young performers!

ANGRY WOMAN, ANDROGYNOUS GOD: *Chitra Sukumaran*

Chitra Sukumaran

Among many firsts for the Kerala state, like adult literacy, woman's rights and public health, — a lesser-known fact is its serious accent on performing arts. For dance alone, competitions are held every year to select the best performers in Bharatanatyam, Kathakali, Kuchipudi and Mohiniyattam at *school* level, then at *district* level and finally at the *state* level. Annually, International Acting Laboratory is held every December, where hand gestures, leg movements, facial expressions, acting skills, yoga and traditions are taught and shared by national and international experts. Details of eye exercises are analysed at the minutest levels by such stalwarts as Keezpadam Kumaran Nair, — integrating them with Kathakali and Kudiyattam as guided by Amanur Madhava Chakyar and Peruayur Kurri Chakyar, last of the living legends. These labs are followed by lengthy performance sessions, such as, 10-day festival of Kudiyattam.

The impact of such sustained exposure to workshops and exercises is evident in the *Abhinaya* aspect of Mohiniyattam, performed by Chitra Sukumaran from Kochi. In the long, musical poem *Gandhari*, composed by the thespian and composer Kovalam Narayana Panikkar, here is a beauteous princess, especially brought from Gandhara for marrying into the Kaurava clan, who discovers, on her nuptial night, her groom Dhritarashtra as blind from birth. More angered than grieved, she ties a cloth round her eyes: vowing never to see again. When she, later, gives birth to her progeny, it turns out to be a lump of flesh. Torn by angst, she hacks the lump into hundred pieces, from which are born her one hundred sons. The latter grow up to be unruly and even sinister, as evinced by their behaviour in the game of dice where Draupadi is insulted and assaulted for no fault of hers. So, finally, when the warring cousins seek her blessings, she says merely: *Yathodharma Stathojaya*, prophesying victory for the true and the righteous. Chitra's execution was marvellous.

In the other *abhinaya* item *Kuttichelam*, also composed by Panikkar, she depicted the manifestation of Shiva as the androgynous god, — before Kannagi, the embodiment of Durga, in the only temple dedicated to her in the south at Kodungallur. The story is out of the ancient Tamil classic *Silappadikram,* but it also connects to an even earlier treatise, *Pancha Marutam,* that outlines eleven dances, of which *Kuttichelam* is one. Again, Chitra's rendering was picture-perfect. Says she, "The choreographic climate in Kerala is fiercely competitive, yet it provides wonderful opportunities. One has to start really early, as I did when I was 9. After more that two decades and a half, I can't say I've arrived. But I think Panikkar, who penned these two pieces especially for me in 2002, has blessed me. I also think I should continue primarily with *Abhinaya*, which I've soaked up so much."

AMBROSIA FROM ACADEMIA: *Deepti Omcheri Bhalla*

When Deepti Omch eri Bhalla presented recently her enchanting Mohiniyattam, it was hard to believe that five monumental volumes on *Indian Music and Allied Arts* were already under her belts, besides two edited compendiums: *Gleanings in Indian Music* and *Immortals in Indian Music.* This was, incidentally, the new occasion when she released yet another insightful tome: *Vanishing Temple Arts*, delineating temples of Kanyakumari district.

"My mother Leela comes from this area, which is now part of Tamil Nadu," Says demure Deepti, who has done her doctoral work on Sopanam music of Kerala and now, holds a professor's chair at Delhi University. "She belongs to a family that held custody of the temples of Thiruvattar, Suchindram, Paarassaala, Tripparappu and Thiruvananthapuram. This was indeed a special privilege!"

Deepti Omcheri Bhalla

The mind rushes back to the 1950's when Dr. Leela Omcheri was herself researching on *Sangeeta Chandrikai* and attempting compilation of indigenous *Ragas* and *Talas* of Kerala, aided by her husband Prof. Omcheri Pillai. Most of that music was already part of a dying heritage. "A gifted singer herself, my mother imparted in me her love of music which was organically linked to dance," recounts Deepti. "Till the 14th century, all three aspects of G*eetam* (music), *Vadyam* (instruments) and *Nrityam* (dance) were well-integrated as *Touratrika* (threesome) in our culture. Even today, Manipur has *Pung Cholam* where drums and dances go together. Kerala still has Edekka, the drum, playing all seven notes and danced with. We call this *Katipadi Sewa*, the service with playing, singing and dancing."

Little wonder, therefore, that Deepti was handed down ambrosia, the delectable repast of both music and dance by her mother. In addition to music, she trained in Kathakali for 12 years from disciples of guru Gopinath. Recalls Deepti, "By 1974, I realised that to be a soloist in Kathakali would be difficult for a maiden. Mohiniyattam was the next best option and, fortunately for me, Guru Kalyani Kutty Amma came regularly to Thiruvananthapuram. I discovered soon that I was learning *Sollukottu, Swara-Jati, Pada-Varnam* and *Tillana,* all poor cousins of Tamil Bharatanatyam!"

Thereby began her quest for Kerala's own Mohiniyattam. "I stumbled upon a musical genre *Vaadil Thuva Pattu* that literally opened doors for local *Javali* (romantic song). By 1978-79, I found Malayalam *Javali* and old *Tillana,* which had more words and notes than the syllables, unlike syllable-loaded Tamil *Tillana,*" avers Deepti. "My foray into *Tala* opened wholly traditional metres like *Raj Vidtyadhara Talam,* also called *Dunduvi Natya,* having six elements (*Shadanga)*: *Adrutam*, *Drutam, Laghu, Guru, Plutam* and *Kakachhandam:* with only a few used in Bharatanatyam. Then there were *Guru Jhampa Talam* (used in *Nritya Prabandham*), *Muddakim Talam* (incorporating

Jati) and *Pani Talam* that would go on and on, in the true Sopanam style! Even the folk-based *Mayul Peeli Tukam* (peacock feather dance) was available."

It all seems a voyage of discovery! Agrees Deepti, "The exciting part was the re-mapping of Mohiniyattam from its debased folk idioms. Before 1930, old nuggets of Swati Thirunal had fallen into disuse. Instead, *Kalabha Kottu* (sandal-paste anointment), *Mookuthi* (nose-ring) and *Kathiraliyum* (nature's beauty) pervaded the repertoire. Guru Gopinath's wife, Thanaknai, who was a great dancer but not permitted to practice in public, gave me a feel of these folk forms. After 1930, the poet Vallathol began resuscitating Mohiniyattam and much of Thirunal compositions returned with glory. We have unearthed enough compositions to make *Nritya* more important than *Natya* and strike a balance between dance and *Abhinaya!"*

DANCING DIVAS OF ANOTHER ERA: *Nangiyar Koothu*

In Kerala, marked by a matrilineal society, it is no wonder that there is a surviving ancient dance-form that evolved from the simplicity as well as assertiveness of Kerala women! The dance-style of Nangiyar Koothu, in fact, internalises those very feminine features and reflect them in the eyes, hands and of the female dancers that have remained — against heavy odds – as an integral part of Kudiyattam, the oldest living tradition of theatre in the world, which is now recognised by UNESCO as a 'Masterpiece of Oral and Intangible Heritage of Humanity'. Performance-opportunity of these Sanskrit plays was always rare. The solo performance of Nangiyar Koothu, and its family-counterpart of male Chakyar Koothu, evolved as a way to express the ability and talent of those performers for whom theatre was a means of livelihood. Nangiyar Koothu was, for long, confined to the four walls of Kerala temples and its acting manual, *Atta Prakaram,* known to the outside world only two decades ago.

Krishna: Festival of Nangiyar Koothu, presented a colourful recapitulation of many gems of this genre drawn from its fountain-head, *Sree Krishna Charitam,* — under 'Rangasree' from Thiruvananthapuram, by Guru Margi Sathi and her two talented disciples: Aditi Gopalakrishnan and Coralie Casassas. Accompanied by *Mizavu* (big drum), *Timila* (small drum) and *Edekka* (decorated drum), besides cymbals, Aditi set off her *Krishna Lila* to depict Krishna as a child. True to her form, she began with *Sabha Neerikshana* (surveying the gathering), *Sangshepam* (summarising the narrative) and *Kamala Parivartana* (lotus-like gestures to mark narrative-changes) and launched her *Ekaharya Abhinaya* (solo performance for multiple characters) with great élan. Playing in mud and dust by Krishna-Balarama the toddler-duo; holding unsuccessfully the cow by its horns; stealing curd and butter; deceiving friends by persuading them to close eyes by Krishna who thereupon ate all the fruits gathered; and the mud-eater Krishna's revealing the Universe in his mouth to mother Yashoda had Aditi displaying her consummate *Netra Abhinaya* (eye-expressions) and *Hasta Abhinaya* (hand-gestures), excluding somewhat *Padakshepam* (foot-movement).

"I'd learnt Kathakali from 'International Centre for Kathakali' for four years and spent summer-breaks in Kerala since I was 15," reminisces Aditi, now 22. "I fell for Nangiyar Koothu, which I learnt taking a year off after graduation in the true *Gurukul* style! *Bhava Abhinaya* (enacting emotions) with face and hands was what I wanted to excel in. I propose to keep this ancient art as my vocation alongside studies and concentrate on themes within the paradigm of Nangiyar Koothu at present." On coming out of solo format favouring group choreography, she avers, "My form is very powerful on *Abhinaya* with which I want to reach people. Getting into dance-drama would make it synonymous with Kudiyattam."

Coralie, the statuesque French danseuse, demonstrated *Puthana Moksham* (Deliverance of Puthana) with considerable verve. Her strengths were more on *Hasta Abhinaya,* a lot of *Padakshepam* and many dramatic pauses and turn-around. Her solo performance comprised Kamsa's ruthless command to eliminate all babies from Vrindavan; merciless paedocides; her changing into a pleasant guise; falling for Krishna's lovely visage; overcoming affection and anger to suckle the divine baby with poison; and final gasping end by Krishna's deadly suction of her breasts. *Ekaharya Abhinaya* was seen in the blue god's feigned slumber and wreaking vengeance on the demon. Coralie's *Bhava Trayam* (triad of simultaneous emotions), with adoration of divinity, recall of Kamsa's wrath and awareness of her own plight, was superbly etched. Says the 25-year-old accomplished dancer, "I'd completed 5-year Masters in theatre-performance from Besancan University that teaches the world's arts: particularly Asia's, specialised in 'ethno-scenology', learnt Kathakali from Martin Chemana and spent six months in Kerala to soak up Nangiyar Koothu that I'd dream of. I've now begun a doctoral programme on Kudiyattam and Nangiyar Koothu under Margi Sathi, after teaching myself Malayalam." Bravo!

Margi Sathi

Margi Sathi depicted *Raasa Krida:* with Krishna's dalliance with milkmaids in Raasa dance. .Sathi had performed here earlier and was at her usual best showing many nuances and delicacies of *Ekaharya Abhinaya.* Adds she, "*Atta Prakaram* is a practical treatise for us, unlike theories described in *Natya Shastra* and *Abhinaya Darpana.* Our source-book *Sree Krishna Charitam* has enough episodes that can last 4-hour daily-enactments over 40 days! It's true that Nangiyar Mouth's power lies in solo performance, but it has enough room for dramatic action, as seen in *Kamsa Vadham* (Slaying Kamsa) with rip-roaring *Patappu-Rappadu* (preparation for battle)!"

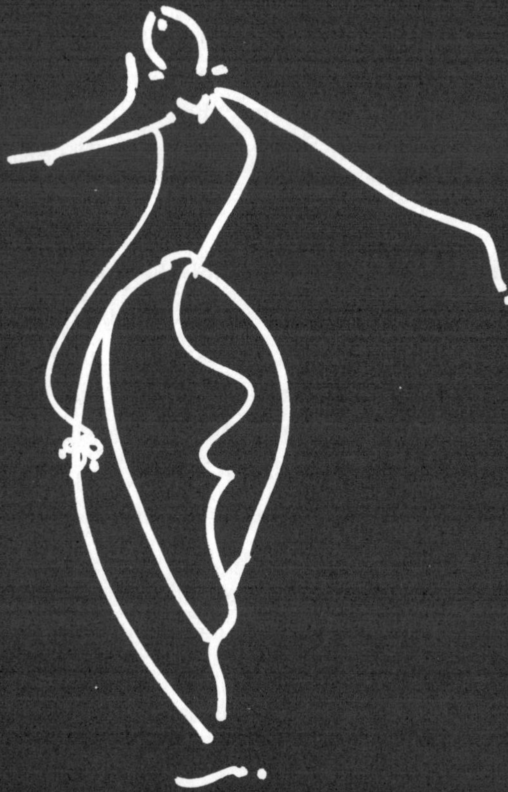

Kuchipudi

Overview

by Vanashree Rao

Vanashree Rao

The success of Kuchipudi, as one of the major Indian Classical dances and capturing the imagination of all — irrespective of any regional division — has been a little lacklutre in the last few years. It is also true that the overall growth of Indian classical dance in terms of dedicated performers, teachers, gurus and also thinking scholars is not very exciting or encouraging, given some major practical problems faced by younger generation of dancers. Still one cannot deny that platforms for performances have increased manifold and individual effort have sustained the dance forms against all odds.

In Kuchipudi, one cannot but link the progression and regression with the past. One need not go into the history, as students of dance or scholars are aware of it, nor is it relevant to talk about individual achievements as it is a tradition in India that artists survive on their own merits, rather than with institutional, organisational or social effort, although there is a lot of indirect support from different governmental and private organisations, if one knows how to acquire such help. This is vastly different from the Western art scene, where, for instance, thousands of artists are earning their livelihood with dignity in the opera house of even a small country like Finland.

Kuchipudi is not a very popular dance form. Eager students do not rush to learn Kuchipudi; they would rather go to a popular style. While, say, Odissi has progressed by leaps and bounds in the last few years, with cohesive efforts made by a large number of performers, teachers and scholars to streamline the form in its totality, — people are still confused about the identity of Kuchipudi. Primarily a dance-drama form, Kuchipudi was performed with simplicity and in rustic atmosphere, and named as a classical form only around 1958. Today, it should have been well-established like Bharatanatyam or Odissi, but the demand for Kuchipudi continues to be less than any other dance form.

There is no clear-cut view of the artists, gurus and scholars as to what exactly is the identity of Kuchipudi. Is it female impersonation: the primary tradition popularised by Vedantam Satynarayan Sarma, or, is it a dance-drama tradition in the period style as made by Vempati Chinna Satyam in Chennai? Was the latter largely responsible for making Kuchipudi firmly classical, by following strictly the tenets of *Natya Shastra*, or the traditional *Andhra Natyam*, or the *Natyamela* tradition, even now popularly known as the Mellatur *Bhagavat Mela*? Or, is Kuchipudi the most convenient solo or duet tradition, as it is practically impossible to produce dance-dramas in a place like Delhi? In no other dance form, these confusions prevail. Though there may be different *Gharanas* of gurus, the other styles may vary due to technical differences, but retain uniformity in repertoire, music, costumes and content, thus making it easy for anyone to follow their steady progress. But in Kuchipudi, all the above-mentioned traditions differ from each other.

Regarding the original female impersonation in Kuchipudi, this tradition is heading at present towards extinction. Firstly, females have now started learning Kuchipudi, and, in fact, the trend has been reversed by V.C. Satyam by even training females into performing male roles! When females with good personality are ready to dance, why should one go to such lengths as impersonation? The whole artistry of a man impersonating as Satyabhama is not novel any more. Unless supported by art-lovers, government and the audience, this genre of Kuchipudi may not be seen in the future. The *Natyamela* tradition is still alive, not all over the country, but to some extent in Andhra and Tamil Nadu, though artists are finding it difficult to earn livelihood from dance. Especially hit hard are the male artists who are usually not invited to perform, unless accompanied by either a female partner or a group of dancers. They look for opportunities to teach abroad, or take up a job in an institution's dance department. Fortunately, Hyderabad University has Kuchipudi faculty.

The original Brahmin families in Kuchipudi village are still teaching there, aided by the Government. of Andhra Pradesh, but there is absence of good performers, as revealed in the younger generation. Those who want to take dance as their p rofession, are burdened by economic factors, lack of infrastructure in providing professional knowledge, inability to communicate to the modern audience and sometimes, brilliance of individual talent is marred by raw, untrained group dancers. Anyone who has seen 'Nrityagram production will find Kuchipudi village production lacking in teamwork and stagecraft, so necessary for making a mark on today's audience. There is definitely need for improvement as we are competing with the best in the country, if we want our art-form to flourish!

Lastly, here is an appeal to all Kuchipudi artists, gurus and scholars to come together and seriously reconstruct this rare art form, without dividing the north and the south, with respect for each artist's contribution, so that we can build a common forum to project this rare form in all its splendour. We need trained artists who can communicate with all kinds of audience, and put forward the distinctive flavour of their style. Without changing the technique, or the content, overall improvement in presentation, with proper costume, lighting, stage décor is a must for today's audience.

Meenu Thaku

NINTH MOOD OF A MAIDEN: *Meenu Thakur*

If one thought that Bharata's *Natya Shastra* was all about the aesthetics of the fine arts and performing arts that it covered, including music, dance and drama, — one should think again. This hoary treatise of the 2nd century did not merely go into the basic representation of words, gestures and temperament of heroines, but also the physical graces of women for whom 'feeling generates emotion, and emotion leads to passion'. If this were not enough, heroines exhibited eight moods and were accordingly named: *Vasakasajja* (one adorned for physical intimacy); *Virohotkanthita* (one distressed due to separation); *Swadhina Bhartika* (one dominating the lover); *Kalahantarita* (one estranged due to lovers' tiff); *Khandita* (one annoyed with the lover); *Vipralambha* (one spurned by the lover); *Prosita Bhartika* (one with the lover in exile); and the glorious *Abhisarika* (one on tryst to the lover). And the initial *Vasaka* was explicitly for conjugal union: on specified days after the 'periods'; to get progeny; for sheer novelty; in queen's absence for childbirth;; during sorrow; or just for pleasure. These then were *Nayikas*: exalted and eulogised!

Nayika: Representation of A Woman in Many Moods of Love was a depiction of femininity in eight amorous stages, by the talented Kuchipudi danseuse Meenu Thakur. Says Meenu, who inherits dynamism from her Rajasthani father, charm from her UP mother and ample grace from both, "Every woman has a bit of the *Nayika* inside her as part of her latent moods and is waiting to give it expression! It's relevant even today when you can discover traces of such passions in varied positions of life. If Satyabhama felt jilted by Rukmini in Dwapara era, won't a contemporary girl feel the same if her boyfriend is snatched away?"

Meenu's *Vasakasajja* showed a swing of moods from desperation to determination, to the tune of a Khestrayya *Padam* in *Raga Pantu Varali. Virohotkanthita* followed a Surdasi Bhajan in *Raga-Malika,* when the *Nayika* is wandering like a bard, seeking Krishna and crushing herself in loneliness. *Swadhina Bhartika* was set to another Khestrayya *Padam* in *Raga Kalyani,* while *Khandita Nayika* resented her lover's attachment to another, in a traditional *Javali* in *Raga Kedara Gouda. Vipralambha* used a Jayadeva *Ashtapadi* in *Raga Charukesi* to express the deceit faced by the woman despite a message of confirmation. *Kalahantarita* was an excerpt from *Bhama Kaplapam* in *Raga Deva Gandhari,* — to show the impatience and enragement of the woman due to prolonged separation from the lover Krishna. *Prosita Bhartika* was a delightful departure to a Tagore song: *In the night of fury and thunder, my Intimate One, I am the storm petrel seeking signs of your distant journey across dark rivers*... The finale was *Abhisarika,* interpreting another *Ashtapadi: Sakhi Hey, Kesi Madana Mudaram*...: that revelled in the love-union of a woman and defied all conventions of modesty!

Are the eight moods enough to catch all the nuances of a woman's fleeting moods and passions, mostly centred on one beguiling hero? Promptly comes Meenu's laughing response, ""No, I always looked for the ninth mood of an independent girl who can play around with multiple boy-friends and 'two-time' them as often as not! But I didn't get an appropriate lyric in the traditional repertoire!!"

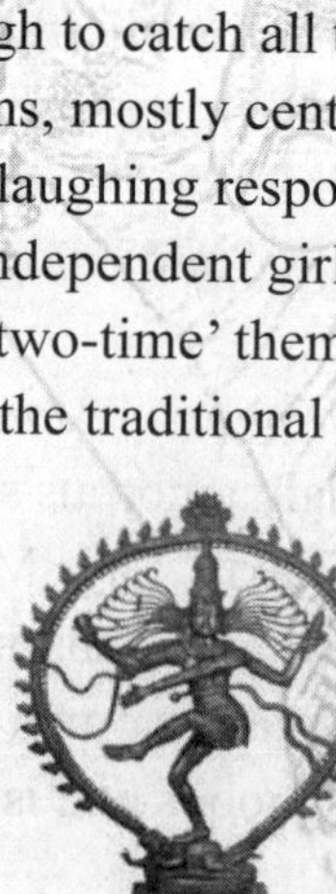

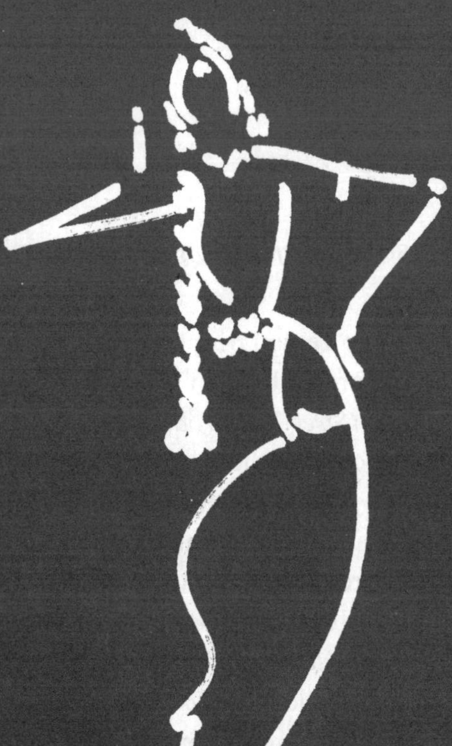

Vilasini Natyam

Anupama Kylash & Sanjay Kumar Joshi

Overview

by Anupama Kylash & Sanjay Kumar Joshi

The cultural history of the Telugu people reveals the existence of two dance-streams: One performed by men *(Purusha Sampradaayam)* and the other by women *(Stree Sampradaayam).* References to *Stree Sampradaayam* abound in the archival, epigraphic and literary sources, establishing the artistic presence of female singer-dancers in temples, royal courts and public theatres, certainly from the 10th century AD. They were referred to by various terms including *Swamini* and *Bhogini,* (colloquially, *Saani* and *Bogam)* with the troupes termed *Chinna Meylam* or *Nattuva Meylam.* By the mid-20th century, these artists were called the *Kalaavanthulu*, a term which derives from *Kalavati (*a woman who excels in the arts). When the anti-*Devadasi* Dedication Act was passed, the consecration of singer-dancers in temples was banned and the art of the *Kalaavanthulu* began to decline. *Saani*s and *Bhogam*s were banished from the mainstream social life.

Vilasini Natyam represents the ritual, ceremonial and operatic-dance legacy of this group, some of whose last living artists have taught the present-day dancer Swapnasundari. This art differs in technique from the *Purusha Sampradaayam* which evolved into Kuchipudi. Though Vilasini Natyam movements appear as quintessentially feminine, it's nearly one hundred *Adavus* (dance-units) include the *Tandava* (masculine) and *Lasya* (feminine) aspects. Vilasini Natyam's complex *Abhinaya* is widely acknowledged. It's extensive repertoire comprises temple- dances, court- dances and dance-operas of the Telugu hereditary female singer-dancers .

The following are some vital requirements of formal Indian dance-systems, some of which were described as "classical" dance-styles after the advent of the English language:

- *Aalaya Sampradaayam / Gudi Seva* (three aspects of temple-service);
- *Anga Bhogam:* Song-dance offered as an integral part of the *Agamic* worship primarily for the pleasure and appeasement of the deity;
- *Ranga Bhogam*: Song-dance concerts that could be witnessed by worshippers visiting the temple;
- *Aata Bhagavatham*: All-night operatic plays performed within the temple - courtyard during major temple festivals, for educating and entertaining the pilgrims. Though their context differed, the same dance - technique was employed for these aspects.

Vilasini Natyam's temple-repertoire comprises *Meylukolupu* (wake up dance-songs); *Baala-Bhogam (Nritta* sequences like *Pallavis,* danced after the initial meal is offered to the deity); *Bali-Harana (*ritual dance accompanying the offer of sacrificial homage to the *Ashta-dikpalakas* i.e. deities who govern the eight directions); *Pallaki Seyva (*dance performed in front of a moving palanquin carrying images of the temple-deity); *Kumbha Haarathy,* (waving of the pot-lamp to ward off the evil-eye cast upon the deity); *Heccharika (*action-song heralding the palanquin's re-entry into the temple). Further, *Japa Hasta-mudra*s (meditative hand-gestures) earlier used by the *Telugu* temple-dancer in the ritual-dances, have been retained in Vilasini Natyam which is presently re-integrated with live worship.

The above rituals, which were once the prerogative of consecrated temple-dancers, are presently performed inside a living temple by female and male Vilasini Natyam dancers. The near-obscure original *Churnikas* (Sanskrit stanzas) and *Talas* (rhythmic metres) pertaining to these have been reclaimed and restored to dance-worship after a lapse of nearly 80 years during which only nominal *Mantra* chanting by the priests has continued. This landmark achievement has been sustained in Vilasini Natyam now for over a decade.

For stage-performance, these ritual dances have been modified while retaining important components. The *Mantra*s chanted by the vocalist are depicted in *Abhinaya.* Elaborate *Tala* expansion now embellishes the earlier *Pallavi*s. The repertoire of *Aasthana Sampradaayam / Kaccheri Aata* evolved from the *Ranga Bhogam* (concerts in a temple): The dancer of yore performed *Pushpanjali, Kavitthvam, Varnam, Padam, Javali, Adhyatma Ramayana Keertanam, Ashtapadi* and *Shlokam* facing the sanctum. The audience of worshippers could watch the concert, which lasted many hours. The temple singer-dancers were required to welcome royalty during their temple-visits. On such occasions, the ruler's virtues would be extolled through compositions like *Salaam-Daruvu*s.

Kaccheri Aata (concerts in royal assembly temple): Temple-dancers were also invited to perform in the royal-court on special occasions. Some were given full-time employment as *Raja-nartakis* (court dancers).A few of them could retain the temple connection, if permitted. The *Varnam* developed fuller dance-treatment in *Kacheri Ata.* In the royal assembly, learned members of the audience could challenge the dancer on any aspect of her interpretation. Initially, *Nritta* was minimal in *Varnam* which a dancer was required to sing, interpreting some portions through *Abhinaya* performed in a sitting position. *Man dharma* (spontaneous improvisation) remained a compulsory requirement.

Many unique *Varnams* of the *Telugu* temple and court-dancers are presently unavailable in published form. *Abhinaya Swayambodhini* gives the text of some *Varnam*s but without musical notation. Fortunately, *Varnam*s have survived as oral tradition amongst the descendants of the *Saanis and Bhogams.* Nearly all of these have been recovered for today's Vilasini Natyam performances and more *Nritta* has been added. The seated *Abhinaya* and *Man dharma* features are retained.

Padam is central to *Kaccheri Ata*. The *Abhinaya* of the *Telugu Saani*s is extremely detailed. Each word and sentence of the lyric is etched, then the whole *Padam* is extensively elaborated, taking up to an hour! Sanskrit *Shloka*s are treated similarly. The *Telugu* singer-dancer employs such *Rati-hastas* (symbolic hand-gestures representing conjugal love*)* which are not currently seen in other traditions. These are incorporated in appropriate sequences in Vilasini Natyam.

Aata Bhagavatham (dance-operas) were performed in the temple-courtyard to entertain the pilgrims during special festivals, after the main worship-rituals were concluded. This extension was added to the temple-dancers' repertoire around 300 years ago. Their popular dance-operas like *Parijatam* and *Golla-Vesha Katha* came to be called *Bhama-Kalaapam* and *Golla-Kaalapam.* The former depicts Satyabhama's emotional states vis-à-vis Krishna in a glorious expansion of *Shringara Rasa* (conjugal love), while the latter is a complex *Vedantic* (philosophical) discussion between a milk-maid and a Brahmin.

Vilasini Natyam retains the characteristic *Margi* (formal) and *Desi* (regional) combination present in *Aata-Bhagavatam* music. The typical *Ganiyam* (light-weight gilded wooden ornaments), which distinguishes the costuming for *Aata Bhagavatham* has been revived. Interestingly, the links between the *Kalaapam*s of the *Kalaavanthulu* and those of *Kuchipudi* have not been clearly and conclusively established. Vilasini Natyam endeavours to project in an educative and aesthetically appealing way the ancient female dance-tradition which was in practice throughout theTelugu-speaking Southern India. It strives to popularise the rich features of Stree *Nrithya-Sampradaayam* in a comprehensive manner.

UNRAVELLING A TEMPLE TREASURE: *Swapna Sundari*

Vilasini: Devadasi Dance Experience, the three-day festival that included performances, demonstrations and seminars, was a courageous effort to put on firm pedestal an almost lost form of ritual dance from the Andhra temples, especially from the coastal region. "In past centuries, worship-rituals were considered incomplete without sacred dances, which were performed only by temple-dancers, known in Telugu as *Saanis* and *Bhogams,"* notes Swapna Sundari, the main architect of researching and recovering this art form from some of the last living artists of this tradition. "In British-ruled India, a ban was imposed on the performance of worshipful dances in temples. With the help of the scholar Dr. Arudra, I tried to revive ritual dancing in its true sense, — re-linking it with temples: once the forum of diverse artistic activity. Thanks to our initiative of re-aligning temple-rituals with worshipful dances, the 350-year-old temple of Sri Ranaganatha Swamy in Ranga Bagh – 17 km away from Hyderabad – decided in 1996 to introduce ancient ritualistic dances as a regular feature. This is perhaps the only active temple, which re-aligns worship-rituals with dance."

Labelled 'Vilasini Natyam', the resurrected style was produced in three neat packages: Ritualistic (confined to temples), ceremonial (for presentation at royal courts) and theatrical (for concert-platforms as operas). Gifted young dancers – Purva Dhanashri, Yashoda, Anupama and Sanjay, the latter as only male dancer so far, and all trained assiduously by Swapna – took turns on different evenings to present temple, court and theatre repertoires, and excelled in conveying, to an uninitiated audience, the flavour of a resplendent form that was languishing in the recent times. Out of the four, Purva stood out, with her skills exceptionally honed

The devotional repertoire, for instance, began with *Churnika* praising the temple's presiding divinity, followed by the elaborate *Pallavi,*

Swapna Sundari

which accompanied morning repast of the deity. Explains Swapna, "*Pallavis* are of three kinds: *Shabda Pallavi* with mnemonics, *Swara Pallavi* with notes and *Swara-Sahitya Pallavi* with literary lyrics. Scholars surmise that the practice of dancing *Pallavi* travelled out of coastal Andhra as an item of the *Telenga Sampradaya* of dancers, — later adapted to the local dance-practice in neighbouring regions." This is an interesting observation, for, *Pallavi* is the staple today of the neighbourhood Odissi style and one would like to hear from Odissi scholars the other side of the story.

In court repertoire, *Varnam* played the dominating role. The dance represented the heroine, or her charming female confidante, to carry messages to the hero. Says Swapna again, "*Varnam* was a musical composition – and later incorporated in dance – which originated in the Telugu land 200 years ago and was popular enough to travel to other parts of south India. *Varnam,* as a music-composition, was incorporated later into the dance repertoire. Telugu was the court language of Maratha kings in Tanjavoor region for 500 years and Telugu *Varnams* were later re-cast into a performing mould as *Sadir* (later Bharatanatyam) by the famous Tanjavoor quartet. These brothers also composed new *Varnams* in Telugu and embellished the older Telugu ones." Are Bharatanatyam scholars accepting the heritage?

The most enticing part was the theatrical repertoire, where the danseuse became a mythological heroine and essayed the role. "The dance-operas are called *Yaksha Ganam* when done in a group or *Vesha Katha* when executed solo," comments Swapna. "The dancer sings and renders dialogue alternately, besides dancing, and involves a supporting character of Madhavi." Excerpts were presented from the vastly popular *Parijatam,* originally running for many nights, alongside a marathon libretto. Based on the legend of Satyabhama and Krishna, Swapna herself regaled the audience – revealing an extraordinary singing prowess – on the final evening. *Bali Harana* was group-choreography where all the disciples enacted *Dika Palikas* (guardian-deities of cardinal directions) together and offered elements of water, wind and fire. Symbolically, the priest with dancers circumambulated the temple sought continued protection of the holy place.

Sattriya Dance

Indira PP Bora

Overview

by Indira PP Bora

Sattriya dance — with its roots in a vibrant living cultural tradition in Assam — was propagated by Assam's 15th century great Vaishnavite saint Sri Sankaradeva who was a social reformer and performing artist. Performed for centuries in *Sattras* (monasteries) by unmarried male monks as daily ritual, this dance form has been [passed on from generation to generation as a oral tradition. Since 1950s, this dance form has been taken over by a few pioneer female senior dancers who promoted the dance form with the help of traditional gurus and scholars as a neo-classical dance form inside and outside India. But performances outside Assam were very few due to lack of patronage and, as a result, awareness about this beautiful dance form could not be created properly at national level.

In the year 2000, recognition came from Sangeet Natak Akademi (SNA) declaring it among the eight recognised classical dance forms of India. Once SNA stepped in, some much-wanted funds started flowing to boost Sattriya in terms of performances, training and documentation works. The new generation started showing interest towards learning Sattriya seriously as SNA provided exposures at intervals.

The valuable resource materials of Sattriya lying in almost 550 Sattras of Assam are yet to be tapped properly. SNA and centrally-funded Shrimanta Sankaradeva Kalaskhetra of Guwahati have started documentation work of Sattriya dance, music and theatre only on piecemeal basis. Of late, Indira Gandhi National Centre for the Arts (IGNCA) has shown interest and has made plans for documentation of old and valuable manuscripts and texts lying in various Sattras. Suggestions have been given to IGNCA to start documenting old gurus, dancers, musicians and theatre persons immediately as valuable resource materials before they become sick and unavailable. It will be a great loss for Sattriya culture, if these resource persons go away without passing their valuable contributions to the present generations.

Time has come for Sattriya to acquire momentum. The essence of boosting Sattriya culture lies in innovation, creation and enhancement of the existing Sattriya dance repertoire within the basic structure of Sattriya culture, to strengthen Sattriya dance as a classical art form. Besides lack of funding as a set-back for senior Sattriya dancers and gurus to innovate and to do more productive work, the other bottleneck is the lack of proper platforms for Sattriya dancers. It will be difficult to encourage the new generation to continue dance, if proper funding and platform are not made available to them when required.

The movement of Vaishnavism propagated by Sri Sankaradeva in Sattriya culture stresses on spirituality, peace and harmony across religious and social barriers through devotion. Today, the world is seeking alternative ways of combating global terrorism and violence through peaceful and non-violent ways. Sri Sankaradeva's spiritual message is very relevant today. The philosophy of Vaishnavism is contemporary. The dance may be specific to Assam but the message is global – universal peace and harmony. This message of Sri Sankaradeva needs to be promoted nationally and globally. Therefore, various important Sattriya projects should be consolidated and implemented within a stipulated time-frame for development of Sattriya dance.

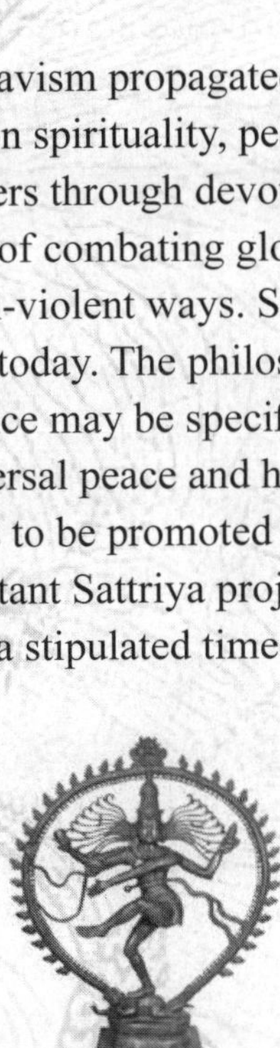

BREEZE FROM BRAHMAPUTRA: *Jatin Goswami*

When the fast-flowing Tsang-Po River, having originated from the mythic Mansarovar and having traversed long through the Tibetan plateau, enters Arunachal Pradesh and then Assam, it is endearingly named 'Brahmaputra', the powerful son of Brahma. But to the valley people, it is 'Lohit' river: more in keeping with its red watercolor. Says Jatin Goswami, the veteran artist who was born and brought up in an Assam 'Sattra' (monastery) permitting married couples, and has lived there in his entire septuagenarian career, "Bereft of Lohit River, Assam would have completely dried up. All our *Janajatis* (tribes) have been sustained by its waters and all our artistic creations inspired by its mighty sight and sound. Would you believe, out of all the Bihu songs that we cherish, eighty percent are composed around this river alone?"

Brahmaputra Beats – a two-day festival on the traditional and folk dance and music of Assam – unmistakably retained the throbbing heartbeats: inherent in its swift currents and echoed the boatswains'

Sattriya Dance

characteristic rhythms: both gentle and virile. Led by Goswami, it began with an orchestral music – redolent of the riverfront tune of *Bhatiyali* in *Teentaal* as well as Bihu beats – with a folk-instrument ensemble: comprising *Bahis* (flutes), *Khols* (drums), *Taals* (large metallic drums), *Pepas* (horns) and *Khams* (large drums). A harvest dance from Gauripuria in lower Assam followed, to the tune of a local Bengali song: *Don't venture, my friend, to fetch the Yamuna water, the mischievous Kanai is lurking there....* The Karbi tribal dance, comprising both plains and hills communities, showed a clear Martial art element: staged before going out to battle and praying for peace and protection of the village folks. Then came a Krishna dance: with an unusual presence of Radha (normally absent in the devotional lyrics of the saint Sankaradeva) that also spoke – again unusually – of *Shringara* (love).

The *Khedai Nach* came from the Bodo tribe (now trouble-torn politically) that put forth devout prayers to Shiva: with rare energy and enthusiasm: with both boys and girls in *Deodhani* style. Especially when the girls let their flowing hair swirl vigorously round the head, it was strongly reminiscent of *Mudiyattam* style from distant Kerala. The Mishing tribal lilt came with its own Paran Bihu melody: seen all along the banks of Brahmaputra: with the petite dancers in colourful 'Mishing Mekhala' costume. From Bada Peta *Sattra,* a celibate monastery that did not permit women, a resplendently dressed devotee-duo sang and danced, with large, circling cymbals, to their god: *Let Hari, our soulful companion, allow us to remain steadfast at his feet....* The finale was *Jhapi* (Straw-hat) dance, a special composition blending elements from Bihu, Bodo, Karbi, Reba and Mising.

Emphasises Goswami, "Melodies of Bihu resonate across plains and hills, and each tribe of ours celebrate Rangali Bihu in April in their own, characteristic style: be it Bodo, Karbi, Mishing, Deori, Morang or Ahung. Our music is drawn from the original sources and costumes are all authentic. Yes, there an incipient Martial Arts tradition in Assam, too, but it has not yet been structured like *Thang-Ta* (sword and shield) of Nagaland. You see, while political turmoil doesn't disturb the artistic expressions, Assam's culture remains isolated, and virtually ignored, from the Indian mainstream; this needs be remedied."

MYRIAD FORMS FROM MAJULI: *Pitambar Dev Goswami*

In the reaches of upper Assam' and within the swirling waters of the Brahmaputra lies the paradise of an isle: Majuli. The mighty river carries the machismo of a unique male-name and brings all the way from Tibet an enormous load of alluvium, — to have created Majuli, all of 700 sq km, as the world's largest river-island! The richly fertile soil is densely covered with woods, and provides a picture of verdant green — with patches of agriculture by its two lakhs of inhabitants and is totally pollution-free, being as yet innocent of any industrial intrusion. In fact, Majuli is, since last year, on the wait-list of UNESCO's sites of 'World Cultural Heritage' for Assam, — a close third after its two game-sanctuaries, Kaziranga and Manas.

But it is not all hunky dory for Majuli, as it gets flooded annually up to one-third of its vast expanse, and an estimated 600 sq metres are gobbled by the hungry river every year. Its seclusion made it an enviable human habitat with many castes of Brahmins and cultivators, alongside Mishmi and Deori tribes. They share happiness and sorrow, and participate together, with gusto, in regional festivals like Bihu. The saint Sankaradeva and his disciple Madhavadeva chose the seclusion of Majuli in the late 15th century to establish some 65 Sattras (places of religious congregation), out of a total of 600 in entire Assam. Says Pitambar Dev Goswami, the *Sattradhikar* (head) of 'Anuiti Sattra', "Earlier, our holy place went under waters four times and it's the fifth time now that we've it re-built!"

The amazing variety of arts that these Sattras carry as their legacy was clear when an exclusive presentation by the artists of Majuli's Anuiti Sattra was made under *Sanskriti Ka Bada Ghar: Majuli* under Dr. Goswami. Explains he, " 'Anuiti' means land of betel leaves; we have a contingent of 600 permanent resident *Bharatas* and part-time *Vaishnavas* who carry on the tradition of *Nam Sankirtana*, living with us since the age of 5. We've above them a hierarchy of three 'Goswamis': *Sattradhikar, Deka Sattradhikar* and *Govindpuriya:* in descending order. Attaining 'Goswami' rungs is by nomination at a very early age, with first entry at the lowest level. While we specialise in Sattriya dance, there're others in Majuli like 'Uttar Kamalabari Sattra' leading in masked dances and 'Chamagudi Sattra' laying accent on puppet-shows." Adds he on the gender issue, "We're all *Udasins* (bachelors) in Sattras, with no women permitted to live here. We, of course, teach Sattriya to girls these days."

While the performance was by no means a finished product, both enthusiasm and energy of the artists from a highly-secluded area – which even many Assamese confess not to have visited — were touching. *Gayen-Bayen* was the curtain-raiser with four *Khol*-players joining ranks with four cymbal-players who doubled as singers. *Sutradhar* was an effeminate dance sans songs and made no contribution to the subsequent drama as was expected. *Dashavatar Nritya* ("he is 63 and has been dancing since he was 6") was surprisingly virile following the opening lines of *Gita Govinda,* but found somewhat repetitive. The best part was the pre-teen boys doing *Natua Nritya,* executing acrobatic postures like peacock, arch, body-climbing, somersaults and yogic poses, with a close resemblance to *Bandha Nritya* of Gotipua boys in Orissa *Akhadas* (gymnasiums), Goswami conceded the evident link, "Sankaradeva was in Orissa and imported the dance. Our Govinda .icon, a close complement to Puri-Jagannath icon, was also from Orissa brought by king Bansi Gopal Dev 700 years ago."

The dance-drama proper, scripted by Goswami, was a sentimental journey through Majuli's heritage. It was a melodramatic narrative, charged with emotion, by male actors some of whom donned garish female robes. From the king Arimatta's endemic tortures which turned Majuli into an accursed land to Krishna and Rukmini's visitation in Dwapara era and declaring the island as 'second Dwaraka', — the mythic events were re-created, followed by celebration of festivals like *Palanam* (5-day *Nam Keertan*), *Raslila, Janmashtami* and the all-time favourite Bihu. Masks were used in *Ankiya-Bhaona* enactments. Avers Goswami, "We've highlighted the rich culture of Majuli, which assimilates the traits of our many tribes in a harmonious whole. Natural disasters and the apathy of mankind, however, have degenerated the world's largest river-island into a pitiable condition." Is the plaintive cry heard in the corridors of power?

A JOURNEY INTO CULTURAL PLURALITY: *Menaka Bora*

Menaka Bora

Blessed is she whose mother dares carry her, Abhimanyu-like, into her 3-month womb, while dancing on a public stage in Assam. Twice-blessed is she when the doyen of Kalakhetra, K. Shankara Menon, gifts her two old sarees (and a blouse) of the legendary Rukmini Arundale, after being enthralled by her Bharatanatyam *Arangetram* at the age of nine in Chennai. Menaka P P Bora, dancing first Bharatanatyam and Sattriya dance the next day, carries many such blessings lightly on her petite, 23-year old shoulder. Gifted with a radiantly beautiful face, chiselled figure and glowing complexion, Menaka began her journey into the dance world when she was a bare 2-year-old toddler and the journey continues when today she is a doctorate-scholar, working on the bonds between performing arts and visual media – after her Masters on global media and trans-national communication – at the redoubtable Goldsmith College (under University of London): known for the humanities liberally mixed with fine arts, music and theatrical forms.

"I'm fortunate to live and breathe an atmosphere soaked with dance and music since my early childhood," gushes Menaka. "My mother Indira started her Kalabhumi in 1982, and has since trained over 500 pupils in Bharatanatyam, Sattriya and other forms of dance." Indira had the impeccable background of Kalakshetra, where she had joined at 13, studied up to post-graduate level, performed in their troupe in India and abroad for 5 years, and yet found time to hone her skills under Vempati Chinna Satyam by learning Kuchipudi. "I never forgot my roots in Assam and was the first female dancer in 1955 in the classical Sattriya form, conceived of by Sankaradeva and practised exclusively by the male disciples of the sacred Sattras in Assam. I was only seven when I danced at the 'Sipoha Satra' at Jorhat," proudly adds Indira.

Menaka's own journey through life was never one-dimensional. While she observed and imbibed a variety of dances since she was 5, and travelled to Chennai intermittently to learn from Dhananjayans and Adyar Laxman in the Kalakshetra style, she also taught herself Tanjore painting and was seriously involved with Hindustani classical vocal. "I was unwilling to join Kalakshetra as a full-time student, although exhorted by Guru Shankara Menon, as that would affect my studies in English literature. I immensely gained from the latter: in my imagery and broadening my concepts," emphasises Menaka. "I always wanted a balanced education in the cultural arena. That's why I went to Goldsmith as its many levels fascinated me. But, most of all, I was fortunate to find the Laban Institute close by. Internationally famed for its work on dance notation, it helped me to focus on my dance vocabulary, offered me courses on choreography and jazz, and provided me a structured approach to body-language."

How has she brought to bear the essential plurality of such learning into her own works? "I've tried to relive history through dance, — in my *Rang-Ghar*", responds Menaka. "This 15-minute solo piece captures the 600 years of Ahom rule, symbolised by *Rang-Ghar* (place of entertainment) at Shivsagar: as a narrative flash-back on the royal bull-fights, swordsmanship, *dola* (palanquin) on the elephant back and ascent on the high grounds. My *Chandralekha* is a 25-minute item on the secret romance between prince Aniruddha and princess Usha, interspersed with the media of live painting (by myself) and theatre. I'm currently working on a collaborative project between British and Indian artists, using visual arts, music, dance and scenography, — and will probably base it on Kalidasa."

What are her dreams for the future? "I believe in an Indian universality, which is basically cross-cultural," avers the young dancer. "My experience and education should enrich my research, with a strong traditional mooring. My view is that Indian classical music is never outdated, but should lead to classical popular, rather than classical elitist environment. It should appeal to doctors, engineers, contemporary theatre people, software professionals and so on, — using modern media of communication, new modes of expression, new treatments of the classical form and a penchant for marketing. TV can play a major role, if judiciously used. I wish to aim at collaboration, rather than confrontation, of cultures."

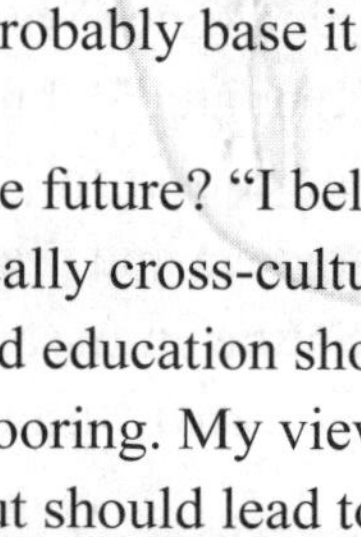

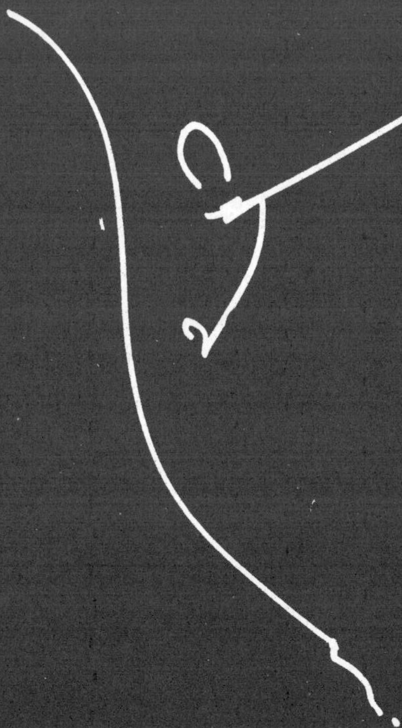

Chhau

Shashidharan Nair

Overview

by Shashidharan Nair

Chhau Dance, the intriguing martial dance form, born in East India, branched out into Mayurbhanj, Purulia and Seraikella styles. 'Purulia Chhau' developed in the Purulia district of Bengal and remains unrivalled in the grandeur of its masks and acrobatic performance. The treasured *Abhimanyu Vadh* and *Mahishasura Mardini* crown the list of items in its repertoire. 'Seraikella Chhau' hails from the Seraikella district of Jharkhand, where charming masks tell the saga of *Chandrabhaga* and *Ratri.* 'Mayurbhanj Chhau' did away with the masks and evolved a highly developed technique in the Mayurbhanj district of Orissa. Chhau was nurtured by its people till it was unveiled before the world and the people outside East India. The Raja of Seraikella composed dances with the help of great masters for a World tour. Guru Krishna Chandra Naik, the great master of Mayurbhanj Chhau, came to Little Ballet Troupe (LBT) in Gwalior under a programme of the Sangeet Natak Akademi. An awardee of the Akademi, he is credited with popularising Mayurbhanj Chhau outside Orissa. Naik created unprecedented ballets at LBT, Gwalior, with the help of Prabhat Ganguly who hailed from the Uday Shankar School. and trained illustrious dancer-choreographers like Bharat Sharma, Bhushan Lakhandri Karna, Shashidharan Nair and Daksha Seth, among others.

Mayurbhanj Chhau lends very well to the genre of modern dance due to its flawless technique and body language that towers above many of the established classical dance forms of India. In Mayurbhanj Chhau, the body speaks. The movement vocabulary, led by 6 *chalis* (gaits) and 36 *uflis* (turns), is inspired by nature. The movements of birds and animals, the sea and the waves, the household chores and the daily ritual of bathing and dressing by the women in the villages: have all been innovatively captured in the movement of the legs, while the hands wield the shield and the sword in the *hatiyardhara* stance. Further combinations and permutations of these steps would lead to an array of new movements. Creative possibilities are limitless and there is always a newness to be discovered and explore uncharted territories with Chhau.

Today, every contemporary dancer is experimenting with Chhau in the metro cities. The leg extensions and the balances are reminiscent of the Western ballet-dance. They blend seamlessly with rivetting rhythms; — forming a compelling bond with nature together with tribal overtones. This approach makes it a mesmerising concoction that urban dancers strive to own. SBKK has produced a significant corpus of ballets in Chhau choreographed by Guru Krishna Chandra Naik's disciple Shashidharan Nair, such as, *Tripurantak, Chakravyuha, Parikrama, Dance of Shiva* and *Shree Durga*. Chhau beckons artistes and *Rasikas* (connoisseurs) towards great artistic endeavours. What is described below is a personal journey with Mayurbhanj Chhau, which also mirrors its recent progress:

It began in 1971 at 'Rangasri Little Ballet Troupe' in Gwalior, where Prabhat Ganguly was the director and choreographer. I was fortunate to learn Mayurbhanj Chhau under the great guru Krishna Chandra Naik who introduced Mayurbhanj Chhau to the world outside Orissa. I was under his tutelage for five years till 1976. During this period, I also learnt a lot of other things, such as, training of the body through exercises as well as improvisation under Prabhat-da who had been associated with Uday Shankar. I had the opportunity to participate in Little Ballet Troupe's first ballet in Chhau titled Bhairavi. *The most interesting aspect was Prabhat-da's innovative ways of incorporating Chhau movements. Little Ballet Troupe has produced many contemporary ballets but each production uses Chhau in a different way, in a seamless manner along with other kinds of movements. Guruji left Little Ballet Troupe in 1976 and joined SBKK in 1981. Circumstances led me also to join SBKK in the same year, where I continued performing and assisting Guruji in the landmark Chhau ballets he created for SBKK, like* Khajuraho, Yayati *and* Karna.

In 1989, I made my first foray into choreography and produced Sangharsh for Sahitya Kala Parishad's Yuva Mahotsav. It was my first attempt to produce a ballet on my own. It was not easy to begin with, but gradually I managed to compose properly. The inspiration came from Prabhat-da and the years I had spent in his exercise and improvisation classes. I realised there was immense potential in Chhau. Mayurbhanj Chhau lends itself very well to contemporary and creative work. One can create and express myriad things with its rich vocabulary!

Gradually, I began to get opportunities to compose ballets for Kendra. Each time, it was interesting to create movements in Chhau. Today my body of work comprises eight ballets for SBKK: Tripurantak, Chakravyuha, Parikrama, Meera, Krishna, Ram, Dance of Shiva and Shree Durga. Tripurantak and Chakravyuha were based in Chhau. Parikrama was a challenge, because the theme was abstract. So I created a lot of new movements using Chhau in a contemporary way. Dance of Shiva and Shree Durga have movements drawn from Chhau as well as movements created to suit the theme. My training in Kathakali under the great master Kavungal Shankaran Kutty Panikkar and a stint with Kalaripayattu with a fellowship from Department. of Culture have helped me greatly in my creative endeavours.

In Delhi, Chhau has become very popular lately drawing people from different dance backgrounds to learn and incorporate in their work. It is now being used for theatre as well. I had the opportunity to choreograph fight sequences in the Chhau medium for a play for Ebrahim Alkazi. I feel that Mayurbhanj Chhau as a form has a highly developed technique, even more than the established classical forms. There are limitless possibilities in the growth of Chhau. My journey in experimenting with Chhau continues. It is a life-long bond!

Santosh Nair

SHIVA AND THE SONGBIRD:
Santosh Nair

Nataraja: the Lord of Dance, presented by 'Sadhya', emanates from the Vedic deity of Rudra: wrapped in many mythologies down the ages. Described as *Maheshwara* Shiva in Panini's grammar in the 6th century BC and Kautilya's *Artha Shastra* in the 3rd century BC, *Rudra-Shiva* was eulogised as a benevolent god in the epics and the Puranas. The human representation as *Uma-Maheshwara* occurred since the Kushana times. The post-Gupta era brought in new Shiva images including *Lingodbhava, Samhara* and *Bhairava Murti.* According to the later Agama treatises, the phallic *Lingas* could be *Swayambhu* (ever-existent) or man-made. The anthropomorphic images were carved artistically from the Kushana period onwards. Shiva, as a master of yoga, music and other arts, was known as *Dakshina Murti.*

Nataraja, produced in dance-drama form, brought forth Shiva in different manifestations. Outlines the seasoned director Santosh Nair, "To us, *Nataraja* is an attempt to thread delicately beauty, grace and energy. It salutes the strength of our culture and, at the same time, applauds innovation. For instance, ours is a reflection of belief in a bonding between tradition and modernity, — a seamless link among the classical, Chhau and contemporary dance-forms: as expressions of our chosen idiom."

Nagendra Haraya Trilochnaya Bhasmangaraya Maheshwaraya / Nityaya Shuddhaya Digambaraya Tasmay Na Karaya Namah Shivaya... began the first scene with *Shiva Panshakshar Stotra,* to view Shiva as a timeless, formless and space less Lord of the Universe. In the following scene, Shiva was visualised as the supreme creator, a source of all dance-movements. While Mohiniyattam and

Odissi explored lyrical element of melodies, Bharatanatyam, Kathak and Chhau used 16-beat rhythms and *Tihais.* Says Santosh, "Our aim was to depict both the moods of *Lasya* and *Tandava,* and show that all movements originated in Shiva. Interestingly, we found that Mayurbhanj Chhau, as danced by the gifted brothers Rajesh and Rakesh — carefully groomed by their father, and Chhau-master, Janmejoy Sai Babu – held their own against any other classical style. It has six *Chalis* and specific *Uflis* and sub-*Uflis* (complete movements) all derived from life." In the vigorous and dramatic context created by Chhau, this seemed largely true and deserved for the latter recognition as classical idiom, with marginal chiselling.

The third scene took up the Shiva-Shakti duality and complimentarity in a highly aesthetic form and created secondary webs around the talented principal duo (Tushar and Bhavini), — almost like the more familiar multiple Radha-Krishnas witnessed in *Raslila.* "Shiva, the ideal lover, is inseparable from Shakti, his expression," explains the director. "The spirit and the material instinct reside side by side – the gentle grace and the powerful nobility." Shiva, in the finale, was viewed as the destroyer of darkness and the redeemer from the fleeting world of illusion. Masks were commonly stuck and then unstuck, — as a show of ultimate salvation, in keeping with the Indian

'Sadhya' Group

ethos. Music and lights were strong points of the presentation, — with glow-drawings of various Shiva *Tandavas* projected as manifestations of Nataraja. "This was with Gobous machine, used to create also the *Linga, Damaru* and Shiva's benevolent feet", brings out Santosh. "Above all, our involvement with multiple dance styles and forms was a highly integrating experience, where we learnt so much from each other .by way of admiring appreciation."

The celebrated character of Nora in Henrik Ibsen's *A Doll's House* is akin to a mockingbird whose trilling notes enthrall everyone: with a small brain-size that contrasts with its capacity to fly over many miles and remember the precise spot where it gathered last the food or the twigs. Nora is a perfectly ordinary housewife who is petted and feted by husband Torvald, and is content to live a small-time existence. But, when the heroic effort she made on the quiet to raise a large loan and save her man — and thought nothing to fake a signature under the circumstances — is terminally challenged by the same man, she revolts. Flying in the face of Torvald, she walks out of her settled household into the cold Norwegian winter and away to her freedom. Even for the drama of contemporary realism that Ibsen had initiated, it was a bold gesture and, as Bernard Shaw observed once, Nora's slamming the door on her spouse shook the doors of the entire orthodox Europe!

Transforming this highly acclaimed naturalist play from its nineteenth-century milieu into an experimental dance-production by 'Sadhya', helped by the Norwegian Embassy, the choreographer Santosh Nair achieved a near impossible feat. As a rule, the Western theatre is like a crystal whose brilliant shine is enhanced by the dramatis personae using the dramatic dialogues as effectively as possible. On the contrary, the Indian performing arts tradition lays all the emphasis on stylisation and abstraction where the dramatic situation is like a prism: — with elaboration of ideas and internalisation of emotions allowed away from the set text. Santosh brought in his characters as dancers, masked men and women, and even puppeteers — interacting with each other and guiding one another to their individual destiny – with maximum abstraction.

The play was done in a total ballet form, supported by evocative symphony music culled from Edvard Grieg, the national composer of Norway. Theatricality was injected with some crisp dialogue retained from the original play: to add relevant context and cohesion to the choreography. The sub-text of Nils (Tushar Kalia), the bank-clerk holding out threats and frustrations, was executed mostly in Chhau movements and provided an admirable counterpoint to the balletic leaps, pirouettes and arabesques of Nora (Bhavini Misra) and Torvald (Karan Kumar). The stage décor was brilliant: with shadow-plays providing the occasional backdrops and the semi-masked men lurking around as members of society. The idea of using illumined cutouts-on-wheels to depict a moving train and showing Ibsen in person for introducing the audience to his dramatic ethos was very effective. Kristine (Rea Krishnatrave), Nora's friend who saves the day for her from Nils, was particularly well-etched in ballet.

"Grieg's music was the determining factor for us and we simply let the dance grow around it organically," says Santosh. "Masked persons as common men and women were used to hold audience interest and to personalize many emotions from the powerful text. We utilised wooden frames to signify traps for Nora who grows out of them finally. The silhouette of letter box and the shredded document were powerful symbols for us in keeping with Ibsen's spirit." But the question remained: why was the play's choreography predominantly from Western ballet with minimal Chhau movement, and not the other way round, as imitative ballet is hardly appropriate for an Indian production? Santosh concedes, "Both Rea and Bhavini are trained in ballet, but still we should perhaps try out the other approach, since our strengths lie undoubtedly in the Indian classical dance and the Chhau idiom, rather than in ballet!

Medley And Miscellany

PASSING SKILLS BY OSMOSIS

Alarmel Valli, the ace dancer, averred in a recent discussion, "The teaching-learning in classical dance should be preferably by *Guru Shishya Parampara* in which transmission of knowledge and skills should be entirely by osmosis". Sonal Mansingh, the Prima Donna of Indian dance – running Centre for Indian Classical Dances (CICD) to teach students — corroborates this with pithy paradigms from scriptures, "A crow's bath is a quick dip in a puddle of water. Likewise, an ideal disciple does not spend unduly long time in bathing and beautifying herself. Her concentration is total, just like an egret looking for a catch, while standing on one leg in the water. A dog, even while seemingly asleep, is nonetheless alert and quick to respond to the slightest signal. Such should be the quick-silver state of mind of the student who is alert to every inflection in voice, every gesture of the guru!"

In contrast, contends Saroja Vaidyanathan, who successfully directs 'Ganesha Natyalaya' and gets, among others, several foreign students under ICCR umbrella, "We follow the Khairagarh University syllabus and give certificates every year. Their course is over in three years, after which we continue teaching for another three years and allow *Arangetram* (first public performance) in the seventh year. It is only after the formal course is finished that the advanced training begins with careful personal nurturing for items, music, choreography and even teaching others."

Sonal Mansingh

So, even considering classical dance as a subtle art, is teaching through modern syllabus a sine-qua-non, or is osmosis good enough?

In the 2-day CICD festival of *Pradakshina: the Tradition of Guru Shishya Parampara,* the question was posed to all three participants, two of whom are teaching dance in the States. Swati Bhise, whose avoirdupois is quickly overlooked, presented a *Ashta Nayika* in *Raga Maika,* followed by all-time favourite *Yemini-Kalyani Padam* of Bala Saraswati: *Krishnani Begani Baro,* which she did for own *Arangetram* in 1980. Says Swati, "I was the very first student of Guru-ji, literally pushing her to teach me! Mine was a process of total immersion: learning *Adavus,* eating query-filled lunches, watching her, seeing her rehearse *Sita Swayamvar,* — a total-learning pursuit. In Manhattan, New York, my Sanskriti Center is a wholly Western institution: with a board of governors, sponsoring Indian artists, holding benefit-nights, organising annually 20-30 sponsored concerts and teaching 75 students with 5 teachers. I've a 5-year syllabus, with theory and practical, and face parents who need things to be clear-cut! Look, I believe in *Parampara,* but today's generation has to be met half-way. You've to allow them to do Disco-dance and yet observe the class-timings, follow syllabus, do *Arangetram* in time, maintain own budget and conduct teacher-student interaction. The sense of communication of our art must not die!"

Meera Krishna, based in Seattle, presented a *Padam* in *Raga Bhimpalasi: Pancha Shakti Sarupini Rajashekhara,* followed by an energetic *Tillana* in *Raga Kannada.* Her hand-gestures tended to get a little clumsy when fast: to be watched over. All of 38 and having learnt for 20 years, she is a believer in *Parampara,* "It's learning all the time: seeing, watching and imbibing. Yes, osmosis is the right word! In the US, I'm teaching 10 students privately; I've to set out a syllabus, define goals and let them know what is expected.. A few students are of Indian origin, some long-settled there and some non-

Indians. My peers – even from different gurus — come and examine them. Such examinations and exposures from elsewhere have helped students get different perspectives. My students, not much younger than me, do express and expect opinions. They like to see themselves in video to do self-corrections." Answering whether ready acceptance in *Parampara* is better than intense quizzing, Meera reflects, "We too, questioned a lot, read books and were encouraged to learn folklores and mythology, visited national Museum and, on the whole, expanded our horizon."

Pallavi Saran Mathur, perhaps the best of the lot and compared to "*Petit* Sonal', put up a scintillating *Varnam* in *raga Shankaravaranam.* Also, youngest of the lot, she had already 16 years' grooming and is opposed to syllabus-based structures. Says she, "Each student of Guru-ji learns at her own pace, as every individual's way of understanding is different. Someone given to athletics would have own kind of *Jatis* (mnemonics) and some others with a mobile face would have own style of *Abhinaya.* By the time of *Arangetram,* we do learn all the basics and absorb them: each according to her own personality. Guru-ji insists on 12-15 years of learning before *Arangetram* and at least 10 years for full comprehension of dance." Does combination of institution and Guru's guidance work best? Counters she, "Students have different capacity and inclination. Some want dance as hobby for interest; some as *Puja* for passion; and some as profession for career. Obviously, the teaching structure has to be separately mapped for each, — to take the art forward!"

There was yet another, very talented young danseuse, Mythili Prakash, performing Bharatanatyam. After a spirited invocation in *Raga Mishra Bhatiyar*: *Jaya Jagadishwari Mata Saraswati,* she executed an exquisite *Varnam* in *raga Husaini* and then a famous *Padam* in *raga Todi: Taye Yoshada,* by Uddukul Subbaiya, where a Gopi complains how, while adoring little Krishna, she got a full kiss on her lips as though from a husband! Based in Los Angeles, Mythili is a product from Shakti School of Bharatanatyam, run by her celebrated mother Viji Prakash., disciple of the great Meenakshi Sundaram Pillai. Given the same question, she contends, "Ours is an art where all the *Adavus, Alarippus, Shabdams, Varnams* have to be based on abilities of individual students who must, therefore, receive individual attention. While bestowing such care, *Parampara* can also be systematised training, on the lines of Carnatic music imparting skills on *Sargam, Geetam, Varnam.* Any system of training is justified that ultimately produce a good dancer!"

The last words must belong to Sonal who quips, "Knowledge, information and learning must be rotated in mind, even among the Guru and disciple. I, too, have learnt much from my students!" Is this a process of reverse osmosis?

Looking Inwards, Outwards & Upwards

Indian classical dances, like other art forms, are primarily about communication. *Bhava* (emotional fervour) of the performer is transmuted into *Rasa* (feeling and sentiment) of the beholder, according to *Natya Shastra* tenets. But does the ultimate artistic perception vary for a performer, — say, from one who is introvert to another who is extrovert? And, are there grey areas in between — left to the spectator to determine — where the performer's emotional state is kept deliberately subdued and not played to the gallery: even when there is ample scope, as for explicit erotica?

Natya Shastra helps a little more by defining *Dharmis* (rehearsed practice) as of two kinds in the dramatic portrayal: *Loka Dharmi* (popularly realistic representation) and *Natya Dharmi* (following stylised conventions). According to later tenets, there is also *Mano*

Dharmi (dedicated to spiritual abstraction). It was interesting to discern shades of all three performative practices in the *Sangeet Natak Awards Festival* enacted by the awardee-danseuses for Mohiniyattam, Kathak and Odissi.

Deepti Omcheri Bhalla was totally inward-looking when she presented Mohiniyattam. After an *Alapana* (invocation) in *Raga Sourashtram* in praise of Ganesha, she launched *Dunduvi Natyam,* based on a 14th century composition, glorifying the rhythms of *Dunduvi* (small drum) which Shiva played to himself during his primordial dance. Set in *Raga Vaidyadhara,* Deepti adroitly illustrated varied rhythmic tempo on an entirely contemplative note: *Sandalwood-mountain wind blow / Spreading passion, / Flowers bloom in profusion / Tearing deserted lovers' hearts...* It was an *Ashtapadi* from *Gita Govinda,* with Krishna's forlorn state described to Radha by her companion and Deepti was immersed in her emotion. The finale was a *Nritta Prabandham,* based on a rare composition on Adi Keshava, the family-deity the Travancore kings. Admits Deepti, "I forget my surroundings and totally become one with my subject. My choreography is pre-set and I was taught by guru Kalyani Kutti Amma to keep my expressions subtle and restrained, and not to overdo my body-movement even for a sensual theme. Flicker of an eye, raising of an eyebrow or tilting of neck should allow the viewer to imagine what I wanted to convey!"

Geetanjali Lal carried forward her scintillating Kathak in an extravagantly extrovert style. After a *Vandana* (invocation) in *Raga Yaman: Govinda Keshava Janardana Vasudeva..,* she reverted to technical Kathak, — demonstrating intricate rhythmic patterns and with intermittent solo flourishes on tabla by the Ganganis: Fateh Singh and Yogesh. It was entirely characteristic of her that her many *Uthaans, Lamchar Parans* and elaborate *Tihais* bore the mark of happy improvisation, followed by a *Thumri* in *Raga Kirwani: Tohri baat ek nahin manahu...* and a Surdas Bhajan in *Raga Yaman:*

Chalata dekhi Yasumati sukha paye...Geetanjali emphasises, "I don't do designed Kathak, particularly in my solo, — having learnt from my gurus to improvise on the spot and reach out to the audience. Kathak has this primal quality of improvisation and pre-designed items leave us bored!" Adds she, "Having been brought up in an intensely musical family and, having decided early to give up my vocalist vocation for a dancer's career, I've been invariably let loose opposite famed tabla maestros whom one meets only on the performance-arena with one's own preparations. Thereafter, it's *Laya-ka-Khel* (playing with rhythmic tempo)!"

Ranjana Gauhar's exuberant Odissi began with an invocation in *Raga Ashavari: Vishweshwara darshan ko chalo man tum Kashi...,* followed by an *Ashtapadi* in *Raga Kalyani: Dhira sameere Yamuna teere basati vane Banamali*... and a Kalicharan Pattanaik composition in *Raga Vairav: Bitila ta jamini*...with resonance of Bade Ghulam Ali's celebrated song: *Ka karu sajni, aye naa balam*... Ranjana veers to the totally outgoing school, "My goal is to communicate without frills and if I subdue my presentation, it'll not be real and *Rasa* will fail to carry itself off! I'm afraid it's ultimately a question of capability and talent, and how much one is able to share. I, for one, don't enjoy restraining myself at all!"

While all dancers easily transported themselves to higher planes for surrender to divinity, one may listen to the academic in Deepti, "Even *Shringara* (love) can be *Madhura Bhakti* (benign devotion), blending grace with sensual quality. I've, for instance, witnessed Kelu-Babu dance Odissi to the last, highly erotic stanza of *Gita Govinda* with the most admirable restraint. You don't have to express yourself explicitly, if you've an initiated audience — expected for classical dance performances – who'd understand every subtle gesture. For uninitiated audience, however, you can possibly be more extroverts!"

SERENITY AND SPIRITUALITY *Rama Vaidyanathan, Rashmi Vaidyalingam, Rajendra Gangani*

A highly-respected critic recently observed that it was pertinent to de-link spiritualism from religion and a spiritual approach to life was far more important to one's own sense of existence than blindly following religious texts and rituals. She even ventured to suggest that the idea of GOD was a reflection of one's insecurity! Put in the context of our classical dances — with such a battery of well-honed techniques and powerful grammar — one is tempted to ask: is it that important to carry still the baggage of the handed-down mythology, imbued with religion, in order to delineate the dance's rich aesthetics to a modern, and largely profane, audience?

When the talented danseuse, Rama Vaidyanathan, used her unbounded energy and enthusiasm for Bharatanatyam, she chose the theme of *Aum: Exploring Indian Spirituality.* In the ambience of a dreaded malady, more concerned with sorrow, sympathy and

Rama Vaidyanathan

Yamini Reddy

downright need for materially alleviating suffering, — was mythology-laden spirituality the best balm that could be offered? Rama has a spirited reply, "I thought that if there were selfless people who were doing conscientious work, I could bring to them in my dance an inner feeling of serenity and peace."

In the process, she used a *Mandukya Upanishad* verse in *Raga Vasanti* to establish that life is the bow, self the arrow and *Brahman* the target, where *Aum* is not God, but an experience to reach God. . Her *Bindu* was culled from *Saudarya Lahari* in the rare *Raga Saramati,* laced with a Tantric text, about the centre and *Shri Chakra,* — depicting relationship between the immortal soul and the outward transient body. Her *Paramatma,* taken from *Bhagavat Purana* and sung in *Raga Malika,* took up Krishna's incarnation as theme and delineated nine different emotions from his mythology. Her *Jivatma* was from *Divya Prabandham* in *Raga Pantubharali* and the final *Shivoham* from *Skanda Purana* in *Raga Chahrukesi.* "In the overall choreography, I've used my dance as medium of communication. My reserve of confidence is my asset and every time I open up Pandora's Box to discover new expressions of dance, such as, the diagonal body-stretching for *Aum* and geometric triangles and circles for *Bindu."*

Tripatha: Confluence of Dance, Music and Literature, organised under Raja Radha Reddy's *Parampara Series* took off with that celebrated duo's Kuchipudi. Mythology happens to be this style's forte and Raja's *Devi Stuti: Prapannati Hare Praseed Devi...,* as invocation to Shakti, was no exception. Following a *Jatiswaram,* with their disciples' neck-movements and scintillating footwork, the dancer-duo presented a Mira Bhajan: *Chalo Mana Ganga Yamuna Teer...* in *Raga Yaman.* Inverting Mira's abstract metaphor, the duo turned it into the mythological *Vastra Harana* where Krishna steals the clothes of the bathing milk-maidens and return them after much persuasion. Says Raja, "I wanted to visualise the nudity and the hand-raising of the desperate *Gopis* as their surrender of pride and ego to the godhead, as taught by Krishna. Water is here a symbol of purity!" and adds, "Yes, it's possible to make the normally *Lokadharmi* (exhibitionist) Kuchipudi into *Natyadharmi* (stylised), as attempted here"

Rashmi Vaidyalingam's *Bhama Kalapam* was another unblemished foray into mythology, where the dancer as Satyabhama describes dramatically the person of husband Krishna to the messenger who pretends to miss the nuances of her narrative, short of her actually pronouncing her husband's name which the chaste lady is unable to do! Agreed that the narrative is full of humour (with such nuggets as: "My husband is my mother-in-law's son" and 'He is in between two brothers") and that Rashmi performed well, but has not the 'Bhama' theme done to death by all Kuchipudi dancers? Rashmi remonstrates, "It's not done on Delhi's stage for last five years and a story — with such palpable fun and wit – offers such scope for theatre, dance and music, which I didn't want to deny the Capital's lay persons!" While Rashmi is welcome to it, this viewer's expectation from her, as an intellectual (she is a practising lawyer) was more!

Pt. Rajendra Gangani's Kathak was impressive, but his choice of themes somewhat naïve. Other than a profuse display of technical Kathak – in 13-beat cycle – he performed a *Thumri: Rangeela Shambhu, Gora Ley Padharo...* in *Raga Mishra Piloo* and a Mira Bhajan: *Thane Kain Kain Kaho Samjhawa...* in *Raga Maand.* Insists he, "In my Jaipur *Gharana,* our elders lay more stress on *Bhakti* than *Sambhoga Shringara. Chuma-Chappi* (kissing and cuddling) are just not for us, as we observe restraint in displaying love in public." So far so good, but has not Kathak moved much farther; in invoking spirituality?

Rajendra Gangani

Seeds of Subtle Choreography

Indian classical dances passed through a cataclysmic *survival* phase around the mid-20th century. To take two major forms, Bharatanatyam and Odissi, in order to illustrate the point, Rukmini Devi picked up *Margam* (set-sequence) passed down by the Tanjavoor Brothers and developed simple 'items' around them: still taught to beginners and foreign students, say, from Kazakhstan. Odissi used *Gotipua* boys in female garb at *akhadas* (play-arenas) to consolidate their physical skills,: still practised. Then flourished the *revival* phase, when Bharatanatyam gurus chiselled *Margam,* created new items and ventured into mythological dance-dramas, besides refining physical accoutrement and musical accompaniment. Odissi gurus formed *Jayantika* conclave to give that style its own *Margam,* embellished with *Abhnaya* akin to Bharatanatyam. Now that the pioneering gurus have defined the dance-grammars, tested out techniques and brought in an all-important stability, the dances are in a *convivial* phase when the 'chosen ones' among ace-dancers can happily attempt their own sophisticated choreography, — without losing grip on grammar and technique, and without necessarily firing from the shoulders of their venerable gurus!

That this is largely true was amply proved in the new choreography presented by 'Nrityagram' of Bangalore. The dream-child of Protima Gouri, that institution is one such crucible where nascent ideas are taking shape under Surupa Sen, with inspired music by Pt. Raghunath Panigrahi and others. 'Kathak Kendra' and 'Kalashram' of the capital are the other two institutions which, while providing professional homes to Saswati Sen and Prerana Shrimali (left since), have allowed the honing of their creative edge par excellence.

Namaskriti was Nrityagram's initial invocation to Ganesha. Born out of extraordinary circumstances, the god with the surrogate elephant-head and trunk was celebrated with rare abandon by five dancers. Says Surupa, "It's composed by Gopal Krishna Patnaik, coming from Ganjam next to Andhra's Telengana, with a southern touch. Ganesha's *Tandava* comes from *Natya Shastra* inspired by the 108 *Karanas* (composite movements) rarely used today." *Aakriti* was a pure dance, inherently lyrical and exploring ornamentation on Orissa's temple-walls in an abstract and geometric vocabulary. *Shiva-Ashtakam* was a depiction of Shiva's many-splendoured glory: with perfect body synchronisation. Explains Surupa, "We chose verses from *Ratnabali* visualising Shiva successively as *Bhairava,* lover Yogi and cosmic walker, *remaining* blissfully unconcerned with his creation. We changed moods through *Raga Malika.*"

The best came from Jaideva's three *Ashtapadis* where choreography reached a pinnacle of aesthetic charm. The first, *Dheera Sameere* in *Raga Des,* was very erotic: *Krishna waits, his flute calls out your name as he wanders through the woods caressing the breeze for your touch*...The second, *Yaami Hey* in *Raga Bhairav,* was Surupa's solo, with the morose heroine wrapped in jealous melancholy: *To whom shall I turn now? My loved ones have deceived me*... The finale was *Kisalaya Shayana,* seldom attempted, in *Raga Vibhas: There is but this moment, I belong to you, make me yours*...Surupa elaborates on the subtleties of her choreography, "I explore 'sacred space': from outside to within, from vulnerable frenzy to absolute stillness. I started with the first *Ashtapadi* crowded with many Gopis, but only one Krishna, where Radha exists because of Krishna. She is a mirage otherwise! In the solo, I worked on myself and pondered over each thought, each inflexion. It's a song of infinite sadness, where the paradigm shifts from *Vipralambha Nayika* (separated heroine) to the lonely soul pining to know: who'll take her over from earth? The last piece exudes sensuality and is essentially Krishna's saga of quest for Radha and is richly nuanced in imagery." Adds she, "As choreographer, I always renounce my ownership of the dance to others, — it's the dancer who owns the dance!"

Prerana presented *Bansidhara-Pinakdhara* based on Dhrupad in *Raga Sohini*, comparing the dancing prowess of two most-loved gods of the Hindu pantheon: Shiva's *Tandava* and Krishna's *Lasya.* The vast proscenium was imaginatively viewed and used as two dancing zones for the two divinities. Then came her major choreographic corpus, inspired by *Parjanya* and *Ap Suktas* of *Rig Veda,* both praising water: *...Then the winds blow, the lightning falls, the flora sprouts and grows, the space overflows, the land readies for the wellbeing ,/ When Parjanya the rain-deity protects the earth by waters...* and again, *The waters that rain in the skies, that spring themselves from below the earth, and that flow in canals, and go towards oceans; / May those divinities of water protect me...*

Prerana used chaste Kathak imagery to create collages, bordering on the abstract. Contends she, "Ours is a water-centric civilisation, where the rivers are held as sacred. I've gone from present to past, covering watery fields, children's frolics, life-and-death on riverbanks and the sustenance of flora and fauna as abiding images. At the end, I've touched upon the receding waters – due to man's avarice — that may bring doom." Adds she, "Beauty and subtlety are hopefully my staples, after I've the language of dance under control. The Kathak vocabulary gives me confidence to express any thoughts I want, like my effort to create aesthetic satisfaction after I've learnt the idiom well!"

Even in a programme on *Shringara,* Saswati could not forsake her penchant for technical Kathak, although she chose a *Bandish*

Raja Radha Reddy

(composition) on unusual 13-beat metrical pattern. Her *tukras, jodas, parhants* and, above all, *tihais* were impeccable, bearing the stamp of a senior artist. But her *coup de grace* was wide-ranging improvisation in *Jugalbandis* with Sunanda Sharma, a gifted vocalist from Banaras *Gharana.* First, it was a *Thumri* in *Raga Mishra Khamaj; Chhabi Dikha Ja Banke Sabaria...,* with freewheeling images of Ma Yashoda, Radha Rani, Gopis and eventually, all devotees. Then came *Kajari: Kahlawa More O Radha Rani...* and *Hori: Rang Dalungi Nand Ke Lalan Pe...*, with the dancer characteristically spreading red *gulal* to evoke the spring mood. Avers Saswati, "My choreography here visualises golden dusk, termed the 'bridal glow' in Bengal, when all beings are seen in their best light, — with the cowherd going to riverbank for a drink, village women gathering to fetch water and the demure housewife watering the sacred *tulsi* plant. As a soloist, I get away form my designs for the group-work, since space-reference to group is far apart from the space-relevance to solo."

GRACE, SOLACE AND PEACE: *Tripatha*

Does seeking God have to be listening to the silence within? Some thinkers are not attracted by silence and feel that they can generally reach the 'spot' within themselves anywhere, even in the midst of cacophony. The young Yamini Reddy, who probably presented the most thought-provoking piece, *Harmony,* in the *Parampara* festival under 'Natya Tarangini', holds a contrary view. In achieving solace and peace, she thinks the most fundamental question that confronts a human being relates to his identity. Asks she, "Am I only the body that will perish after some time and of which nothing will remain? If there is soul in me, where does it reside, how is it and what is its relationship with my body?" She quizzes further, "To explore the essential nature of man, is there anything beyond body and soul? We all worship God in our temples but easily forget that God is not something far away and happens to be very much present within us: as eternal soul: — to provide succor and solace."

Harmony was, innocuously, preceded by European contemporary dance by two simply-dressed danseuse-duos: Leah R Curtis from USA and Nikolina Nikoleski from Russia: to Western viola and other instrumental accessories. In today's post-modern world, such solos and duets have a core of theory and process and a lot of challenging movements that have nothing common with Indian classical dance. Interestingly, the same pair of overseas dancers, in the same costume, transformed themselves to don the role of 'soul' and try to capture their 'body', that is, Yamini. Ignoring the implied irony for the time being, Yamini as 'body' was solidly supported by her 'five senses', — a phalange of five young Kuchipudi dancers, alternately dismayed and daunted, trying to 'claim' Yamini. In a Mephistophelean tussle – in the reverse gear — nobody won upfront, but achieved together a consensus and a balance between 'body' and 'soul' .Emphasises Yamini, who is herself the choreographer, "VC Joshi provided the nucleus some months back, which possessed me ever since. This is 'fusion' for me, if you like, where none of us surrender our essentials and still we achieve a balance at the end."

Ode to Shiva, a solo by Yamini at the beginning, was a virtuoso performance with scintillating *Adavus* (postures) and *Karanas* (total body-formations). The brimful energy-level was infectious, the tempo breathtaking and the occasional pause highly captivating! Yamini admits candidly, "This is my father's piece which I enjoy doing as a complete item of dance. I particularly like its subtle expressions of *Nava Rasa* (nine emotions) in a truly stylised manner." Endorses a visibly proud Raja Reddy, "I've been performing it for forty years, but Yamini has added a lot of grace and vitality due to her supple body and youthful exuberance!"

After Sai Bhavani, who has been providing excellent vocal support in the festival, sang a sonorous ode to Ganesha: *Vakratunda Mahakaya Kotisurya Samaprabha...,* Priyadarshini Govind from Chennai rendered items from her *Margam* repertoire of Bharatanatyam.

Her *Devi Stuti* delineated different aspects of Shakti, followed by a traditional *Varnam,* handed down by Tanjavoor quartet from the 19th century in *Raga Bhairav.* Says she, "I described the magnificent Shiva of the Thiruvaroos temple. I was happy to do a *Javali* next, in a light-hearted note where a young maiden wonders how any girl can overcome her infatuation when she accosts a handsome youth!" *Tillana* was a gem from Balamurali Krisnna's stables in *Raga Behag* and the final *Vande Mataram* was in time-tested *Raga Des.* As a very seasoned dancer, was she not keen to provide something new to the Capital's viewers? She contends, "I think the audience here appreciates my *Margam.* Anything, howsoever traditional but aesthetically satisfying, is my choice. When I performed in the USA a 2nd century *Sangam* poem about the valorous mother who visits the battlefront to check whether her son died of wounds inflicted from behind while fleeing, or sustained from front while fighting bravely, — women were touched by the relevance still!"

Sharmila Biswas, the veteran Odissi danseuse from Kolkta, presented items that combined tradition with her in-depth research. The invocatory *Ramashtakam* culled out prominent episodes from Rama's life –that people fondly remember and enjoy viewing again and again — as a group composition, followed by a Kelucharan Mahapatra classic on *Vatsalya rasa.* Sharmila obviously gloried in depicting, through Krishna-and-Yashoda theme, what the interplay of affection and love would universally be between any mother and child. The finale was *Evocation,* a dance-piece that emerged from her interactions with the traditional *Mridanga* artists of Orissa, —capturing spectators' heart in its finesse and grace. Recalls Sharmila, "This was my first investigative work into the varied sub-styles of playing drums from Orissa's interiors like Daruni, Pala, Ranighati and Sanjhab. I derived so much knowledge from these humble people and collected an amazing lot of material about this folk instrument: capable of such variety!" On choreography, "We seem to be enamoured of the Western concepts of space, use of music, entry and exit when we use that term. In fact, our solo dancers, too, use choreography in their own way. Ours is a narrative heritage where spacing and progression of events are a seamless flow on stage, without the leaps and flairs of the West, but have no less choreographic thought!"

BIBLIOGRAPHY

Bardhan, Gul, *Rhythm Incarnate, Tribute to Shanti Bardhan,* Abhinav Pub., ND, 1992

Board of Scholars, *The Natya Shastra,* Sri Satguru Pub., Del., 1992

Chandran, Geeta & Rajeev Chandran, *So Many Journeys,* Neogi Books, ND, 2005

Chatterjee, Ashoke, *Dances of the Golden Hall,* ICCR, ND, 1979

Chatterjee, Gayatri, *Nritya Darpan* (Bengali), Bamacharan Mukhopadhyay, Kolkata, 1992

Chatterjee,Gayatri, *Bharater Nrityakala* (Bengali), Nava Patra, Kolkata, 1965

Citaristi, Ileana, *The making of A Guru: Kelucharan Mohapatra,* Manohar, Del., 2001

Gandharva Maha Vidyalaya, *Angahar Festival of Odissi Dance, ND, 1985*

Gauhar, Ranjana, *Odissi: The Dance Divine,* Niyogi Books, ND, 2007

Govindarajan, Hema, *The Natya Shastra & Bharat Natya,* Harman Pub, ND, 1992

Khokar, Ashish Mohan, *Guru Maya Rao,* Ekah/Rupa &Co., Bangalore, 2004

Khokar, Mohan, *His Dance, His Life: A Portait of Uday Shankar,* Himalayan Books, ND, 1983

Kothari, Sunil, *Bharata Natyam,* Marg Pub., Mumbai, 1997

Kothari, Sunil, *Kathak: Indian Classical dance Art,* Abhinav Pub., ND. 1989

Kothari, Sunil, *New Directions in Indian Dance,* Marg Pub, Mumbai, 2003

Kothari, Sunil, Odissi: *Indian Classical dance Art,* Marg Pub., Mumbai, 1990

Kothari,Sunil & Khokar, Mohan, Ed., *Uday Shankar: A Photo-Biography*, Ravi Shankar, RIMPA, ND, 1983

Krishna Rao, U.S. & Chandralekha Devi, U.K., *A Panorama of Indian Dancing,* Sri Satguru Pub, Del., 1933

Lowen, Sharon, *The Performing Arts of India: Development & Spread Across The Globe,* Shubhi Pub, Gurgaon, 2005

Misra, Susheela, *Some Dancers of India*, Manohar, Del., 1992

Nair, A. & Panikkar, K., *Kathakali: The Art of The Non-worldly,* Marg, Mumbai, 1997

Narayan, Shovana, *Indian Classical Dances,* Shubhi Pub, Gurgaon, 2005

Narayan, Shovana, *Indian Theatre & Dance Tradition,* Harman Pub, ND, 2003
Odissi Research Centre, *The Odissi Path Finder,* Bhuvaneshwar, 1988
Raman, Shakuntala, Ed., *Rukmini Drvi Arundale: A Birth Centenary Volume,* Kalakshetra Foundation, Chennai, 2004
Samson, Leela, *Rhythm in Joy: Classical Indian Dance Traditions,* Lustre Press, ND, 1987
Sangeet natak Akadem, *Kutiyattam: Special Issue,* ND, Number 111-114
Sarabhai, Mrinalini, *Understanding Bharatanatyam,* Darpana, Ahmedabad, 1981
Singha, Rima & Massey, Reginald, *Indian Dance: Their History & Growth,* Faber & Faber, London, 1977
Skolimowski, Heryk, *Dance of Shiva in the Ecological Age,* Calarion Books, Del., 1991
Swapnasundari, *The World of Koochipoodi Dance,* Shubhi Pub.,Gurgaon, 2005
Vaidyanathan, Saroja, *Classical Dances of India,* Ganesha Natyalaya, ND, 2004
Vatsyayan, Kapila, *Classical Indian Dances in in Literature and The Arts,* Sangeet natak Akademi, ND, 1977
Vatsysyan, Kapila, *Indian Clasical Dance,* Publications Division, Min. of I&B, ND, 1974
Venu, G., & Paniker, Nirmala, *Mohiniyattam: The Lasya Ddance,* Natana Kairali, Kerala, 1987
Venu, G., *Into The World of Kutiyattam,* Natana Kairali, Kerala, 2002
Venu, G., *Kathakali & Kutiyattam,* Natana Kairali, Kerala, 2005

Index

A

Aarati, 79
abhinaya, 19, 22, 23, 36, 42, 50, 73, 74, 85, 86, 90, 105, 107, 111, 118, 124, 135, 137, 152, 154, 156, 179, 180, 183, 184, 185, 186, 195, 196, 197, 224
Alarippu, 60, 95, 96, 225
Amar Chitra Katha, 120
Anga, 42, 43, 56, 65, 78, 115, 195
Arangetram, 45, 71, 210, 222, 223, 224
Ashtapadi, 18, 56, 88, 91, 101, 108, 117, 145, 178, 192, 196, 226,227, 232
Atharva Veda, 92, 140

B

Baijis, 149
Bandish, 83, 126, 130, 145, 233
Bhairavi, 21, 51, 71, 97, 111, 215
Bhakti, 43, 53, 56, 68, 69, 87, 91, 165, 166, 172, 227, 230
Bhava, 42, 43, 44, 76, 107, 135, 172, 184, 185, 225, 236

C

Chandala Vikshuni, 172
Charagh-e-Dai, 133
Charya Nritya, 63
Chitrangada, 28, 105, 112, 172
Chowguna, 134
Chowks, 111
Chuzhippu, 178

D

damaru, 135, 219
Dashavatara Stotra, 90
Desi, 11, 197
devadasis, 22, 60, 73, 100, 112
Dhrupad, 82, 83, 113, 126, 130, 145, 148, 233
Draupadi, 104, 117, 118, 135, 164, 179
Durga, 21, 117, 152, 180, 215, 216

E

Edekka, 173, 174, 175, 182, 184
Eklavya, 87
Enniya Mudial Vendum, 77
Erl King, 154, 155

F

Fana'h, 22

G

Ganga Yamuna, 105, 113, 230
Garuda, 80, 109
Gat Nikas, 127, 128, 130, 136, 137
gharana, 69, 73, 83, 127, 128, 130, 189, 230, 235

Ghungroo, 128, 130, 136

H
Hamsanadam, 58
Hari-Haro, 109
Hastamudra Viniyoga, 108
Hathor, 61, 62
Hindol Sthapan, 69
Hori Khela, 27

I
Indira Gandhi, 26, 104, 204
Ishta Devata, 79
Itminaan, 157

J
Jatis, 60, 82, 131, 224
Jatiswaram, 60, 73, 96, 230
Javalis, 50, 89
Jugalbandi, 75, 139, 152, 235

K
Kali, 91, 111
Kapi, 51, 56
Karanas, 80, 232, 236
Kathakar, 124, 138, 141
Khayal, 83, 131
Kirwani, 21, 104, 108, 226
Kritis, 68, 69

L
Lasya, 81, 82, 86, 109, 117, 125, 149, 164, 178, 195, 218, 233
Lavanya, 20, 42, 43, 44
Layakari, 125, 130
Lokadharmi, 43, 230

M
Maddalam, 174, 175, 178
Madhyama, 70, 75
Madhyamavati, 51
Maha pattabhishekam, 19
Mahabharata, 53, 85, 105, 135, 142, 163, 175
Mahari ang, 20, 117, 118
Mallari, 49, 95
mangalacharan, 101, 109, 115, 117
margam, 17, 31, 60, 74, 88, 89, 91, 94, 95, 96, 231, 236, 237
Margi, 11, 18, 171, 184, 185, 186, 197
Mayurbhanj Chhau, 22, 214, 215, 216, 218
Moksha, 56, 111, 115, 184
mridanga, 49, 63, 71, 81, 90, 91, 114, 136, 237
mudras, 28, 35, 49, 59, 111, 196

N
Natabar, 11, 130
Nataraj, 11, 21, 44, 62, 63, 79, 85, 217, 219
Natya Shastra, 11, 19, 34, 36, 48, 70, 81, 100, 186, 189, 191, 225, 232
Natyadharmi, 49, 139, 230
Nava Rasas, 48

Nayak, 69, 128, 145
Nayika, 42, 51, 73, 92, 96, 128, 191, 192, 223, 233
Nritta, 22, 23, 60, 85, 101, 195, 196, 197, 226
Nritya, 22, 23, 60, 63, 108, 182, 183, 209

O

Olipadaitha Kanninai, 77
Om Namah Shivaeh, 139

P

Padam, 23, 50, 51, 60, 62, 73, 86, 88, 89, 90, 92, 94, 95, 96, 97, 145, 179, 192, 196, 197, 223, 224
Pada-Varnam, 51, 182
Padhant, 127, 130, 136, 139, 145, 148
Pallavi, 105, 109, 117, 195, 196, 199, 201
Parampara, 16, 222, 223, 224, 225, 229, 235
Prabandham, 87, 182, 226, 229
Prakriti-Purusha, 46
prasad / prasadam, 68, 79
Puranas, 52, 172, 217
Puranic, 79, 80, 142, 169
Pushpanjali, 59, 73, 92, 94, 196

R

Raas Lila, 91, 120, 160
Raga Bageshri, 88, 92, 94, 137
Raga Behag, 92, 237
Raga Bhim Palasi, 83
Raga Des, 58, 76, 83, 95, 103, 232, 237
Raga Hamsadhwani, 95, 104
Raga Hindalam, 60
Raga Kalyani, 64, 192, 227
Raga Kedar, 88, 156, 192
Raga Kirwani, 104, 108, 226
Raga Malika, 49, 51, 56, 71, 73, 76, 90, 92, 192, 229, 232
Raga Natai, 73, 88, 92
Raga Rageshwari, 92, 104, 156
Raga Shankarabharanam, 51
Raga Todi, 95, 224
Raga Yaman, 56, 104, 108, 140, 141, 226, 230
Raga Yemini Kalyani, 49, 51
Ragas, 21, 49, 51, 56, 58, 60, 76, 78, 82, 83, 90, 97, 108, 170, 173, 175, 182
Ragas Saveri, 90
Raghu Vamsam, 105, 113
Ramayana, 19, 29, 51, 66, 174, 175, 196
Rig Veda, 149, 233
Rudra, 79, 80, 104, 199, 217

S

Sahitya, 22, 62, 83, 201, 217
Sakhi, 108, 127, 135, 192
Sangam, 18, 27, 51, 87, 127, 171, 237
Shabdam, 60, 96, 97, 225

Shakti, 46, 53, 57, 61, 64, 65, 77, 83, 115, 218, 223, 230, 237
Shloka, 42, 59, 70, 108, 196, 197
Shringara, 46, 51, 69, 86, 89, 95, 97, 98, 118, 139, 197, 207, 227, 230, 233
Sopana, 170, 173, 178, 180, 183

T

Taal , 126, 139, 207
Talas, 101, 178, 182, 196
Tandava, 64, 65, 80, 81, 82, 83, 86, 92, 111, 149, 195, 218, 219, 232, 233
Tantrik, 36, 63, 68, 111
Teentaal, 125, 126, 127, 152, 207
Thang-Ta, 161, 208
Tihais, 97, 126, 137, 139, 218, 226, 235
Tillana, 60, 64, 65, 71, 88, 92, 94, 95, 96, 97, 182, 223, 237
Tukras, 97, 131, 235
Tulsi, 80, 235

U

Upaj, 75, 83, 126
Upanishad, 77, 229
Uthan, 130, 152, 184
Utsava Sampradaya Kritis, 68
Uttama,

V

Vande Mataram, 77, 237
Varnam, 51, 59, 60, 71, 86, 88, 92, 94, 95, 96, 97, 182, 196, 197, 201, 224, 225, 237
Vatsalya rasa, 56, 237
Vazhuvoor, 59, 75, 86, 90
Vedic, 78, 79, 80, 217
Vilambit , 134, 137, 152

Y

Yajnas, 53, 79
Yajur Veda, 79, 80
Yakshagana, 19
Yantra, 46
yonis, 103